Kitchen Table
Goldmine

Kitchen Table Goldmine

How To Make Over $1000 A Week With A Simple, Home-Based Mail Order Business!

Lance A Murkin
Roger Mason

Writers Club Press
San Jose New York Lincoln Shanghai

Kitchen Table Goldmine
How To Make Over $1000 A Week With A Simple,
Home-Based Mail Order Business!

Writers Club Press
an imprint of iUniverse.com, Inc.

For information address:
iUniverse.com, Inc.
620 North 48th Street, Suite 201
Lincoln, NE 68504-3467
www.iuniverse.com

ISBN: 0-595-13607-9

Printed in the United States of America

Dedication

Roger–To my three wonderful kids David, Alicia, and Krista. My HERO'S! And especially to my wonderful wife Kathy without whom my life would be totally unfulfilled.

Lance–To my children Spencer and Samantha who completely changed my life. To Dawn for tolerating all the long hours, helping me 'stuff envelopes', and sharing this experience of life with me.

Contents

Introduction

This book has two authors. Both of us have contributed different sections to the book, but we've always written in the first person to keep it consistent.

The method you're about to learn is proven, it really works–*if you use it*! We've done everything to explain it in a simple, yet powerful way. Take your time with it but take time to learn it and apply what you learn–you won't be disappointed!

When I first began looking for an honest legitimate way to make money from home, I was confused, let down and ripped off more than once. After my initial experience, I can see why so many people fail in their quest to make money from home. But I perservered and that tenacity paid off for me–I stumbled upon an amazing, simple home business that I truly believe anyone can do. Along the way, I discovered how all the scam artists were making their money too.

This book will reveal to you the secrets I uncovered, the system I developed and exactly what I have done. I am giving you 100% of my knowledge, I am withholding nothing. I firmly believe if you take the time, put in the effort and follow my lead, you will be rewarded. I am certain of it. Good Luck and God Bless –

Lance & Roger

Chapter One

The Beginning

SUCCESS LEAVES CLUES

Life is an illusion. A blank piece of paper that your perceptions color. Any limitations, any boundaries that you perceive are your own creation. Take this opportunity to decide once and for all that you will change your life. You will make choices and take action and keep your eyes on your goal. Don't be concerned with possible negative outcome. Stay focused.

Make a very defined, very exact goal and review it everyday. Every morning and every night. Write it down and read it out loud. This will keep you focused on the outcome of your actions.

While it is true, you can only work with the gifts God gave you, the possibility between where most of us are and most of us are capable is so vast it boggles the mind.

Just suffice it to say the winners in life set goals, break boundaries and find solutions. The losers find excuses, problems, and reasons why they "can't". Life is an ongoing choice. The choice is yours.

You've probably heard it before. SUCCESS LEAVES CLUES! It's true, you know. Take a look at every successful person in *any* field you can think of and once you brush away the particulars, there's a certain set of 'truths' that are universal to all of them.

The first one I discovered was the idea of capitalizing on the work of others. I was lucky because when I was a child my parents instilled in me two things that have shaped my life. Number one: You can do *any-thing* you want to do if you want to do it bad enough and Number two: You can find out almost anything you want to know from books. What you want to know is probably written down in a book somewhere. By using the work of others which they recorded in books I've been able to study any subject that I wanted to succeed at. This gave me a real boost to accomplishing my goals in life.

But even before that part of it, this whole business of success starts with a wish. A simple wish. "I wish I could quit my job and make money from home." Well, how much money would you need to make to quit your job? $1000 a week? $25,000 a month? Define it, exactly what you need. Then think about all the good things that would go along with that: Making your own hours, no boss yelling at you, being able to spend more time with your family, unlimited possible income, etc. Make a list on paper. Write down every possible 'positive' that could come from your 'wish'.

Now visualize what it would *feel* like to have it. Imagine (yes close your eyes) not having to get up early, fight traffic¾just having a little office in your house. See yourself relaxed with the very content feeling of know-ing all the bills are paid and there's more than enough money to go around. You've got to really *feel* that feeling.

Okay, so how are you going to do this? We need a plan. What can you do at home to make the kind of money you need? Use your mind. The answer will come. Start looking in some business opportunity maga-zines and keep your eyes open.

You see the little pattern we just described is what I call the "SUCCESS FORMULA". This is the evolution of every successful person that has ever been. It's the common link, the clues that success leaves behind. The only way a wish can manifest into reality is through desire and ultimately belief. The only way to cultivate desire and belief is through creative thought or visualization. It's a proven fact.

So let's quickly recap our "Success Formula":

1. Make a wish and take time to really define that wish. Be as particular as possible.
2. Write down all the positives that will come out of the accomplishment of your wish/goal.
3. Visualize yourself having accomplished your goal. See all the positive things you wrote down happening to you, really feel this feeling.
4. Begin to formulate a defined plan to accomplish your goal. The "plan" may not materialize at first, but with repeated practice it will.

Review the steps *everyday*, once in the morning and once at night. This will create powerful and amazing changes in your life. **BELIEVE IT!** Take this simple plan and put it to the test, even if you have already begun your journey. It will speed you to succeed faster than you can imagine and open doors you may have never discovered.

THE OBSTACLE IN YOUR PATH

Although problems appear to be burdens to us in our lives, they are actually opportunities for growth. In the long run, we really should welcome problems and frustrations for only out of the solutions do we find real growth and happiness.

It's very hard to actually put into practice, I know. It's hard to have a hectic day with two or three major things going wrong and actually go "This is a great chance for me to grow!" Blah!! Now you sound like one of those 'sunshine' people who always see the good side of life. Well, you know they're probably right even though most of us would rather not admit it.

A lot of us even make a life out of avoiding work, commitments, stress, almost anything that might be painful. You ever had a job where you worked twice as hard at looking busy as you would've if you just actually did something? Sounds funny but I know a lot of folks who have. Myself included.

But after awhile, we find ourselves in Nowheresville doing nothing with a bunch of other nobodies who are doing nothing too. And before you know it, your life is just a bunch of coulda, shoulda, woulda…

Sooner or later, we all have to take the initiative and try to confront the problem. Face a little pain and find out you actually can live through it. It becomes a habit after awhile. They say successful people all have one thing in common. They are willing to do what the average person is not. They are willing to take a risk, try to solve a problem or face a difficult decision. And they don't give in to fear.

I'd like to share with you this little story I remember from awhile ago. In ancient times, a King had a boulder placed on a roadway. Then he hid himself and watched to see if anyone would remove the huge rock. Some of the King's wealthiest merchants came by and simply walked around it. Many loudly blamed the King for not keeping the roads clear, but did nothing about removing the stone from the way. Then a peasant came along carrying a load of vegetables. On approaching the boulder, the peasant put down his load and tried to move the stone. After much pushing and straining, he finally succeeded. After he picked up his load of vegetables, he noticed a purse laying in the road where the stone had been. The purse contained many gold coins and a note from the King indicating that the gold was for the person who moved the stone from the roadway. The peasant learned what many others never understand. Every obstacle presents an opportunity to improve one's condition.

WHAT'S THE BIG IDEA?

Welcome to a world where your future is in your own hands. That is of course where it's always been. The book you hold contains a powerful message that tells how you can change your life. How you can fulfill your dreams. And the dreams of your family. It is not the only plan of attack you can use to change your life. There are countless others. Many people just aren't suited to handle many of them, though.

This plan requires one crucial ingredient...common sense. That's right. Common sense. Good, hard, and effectively applied common sense. But it's not the easiest thing you have ever seen, either. It requires a high degree of professionalism. If you think of the direct response advertising business (mailorder) as being something requiring less than a good level of professional expertise, then you are in trouble. I could go on and on, but enough of that (for now).

Our plan is as follows: You write a book detailing how the common man can put his available time and efforts to use to gain for himself the one thing he never has enough of—money. You are going to tell people how to make money. If you can learn to do that successfully by following the principles detailed in this book you will become a very rich man yourself. The market for moneymaking information is huge. It grows in size every year. Money, and how to get it, is one thing that is always on people's minds. I don't believe you could disagree.

Read this book carefully and go over it *several times*. Put your brain in gear and think about what is being said. The method described is one of the most financially lucrative "mail order" ventures there is. It is one where the beginner can succeed on his first try.

EMPTY YOUR CUP FOR SUCCESS

It doesn't matter what information you get, its useless without one ingredient...*ACTION!* Real, honest, good information about how to make money (or whatever your field) from someone who has experience, *is truly valuable*. However, if you don't take *ACTION* and apply that information, it's useless. Plain and simple.

And here, once again, we discover that the secret lies inside ourselves. Purchasing information about your subject, studying and learning all you can, is without a doubt a key to success. However, putting that information to use is the only way to *get that success*! Having a mentor, someone you can ask questions and bounce ideas off of is one of the best ways to get a leg up starting your own business. But be prepared to accept criticism to some of your ideas. You are, after all, just getting started and when you ask for the advice of one with more experience, honor that experience by at least accepting the information, not arguing.

I remember a story about a very intelligent college professor who went to see a great ZEN master to learn all he could from the master about ZEN and about the meaning of life. After traveling many miles to see the master, they sat down together for tea. The professor began to go on at length about all he knew about ZEN and what he thought was the meaning of life. The ZEN master sat patiently listening and the few times he tried to speak, the professor quickly cut him off with his own feelings about whatever the master had begun to speak of.

After a while, the master asked the professor if he wanted some more tea. The professor said, "yes, thank you". As the master filled his cup, he continued to pour the tea even as it run over the top and onto the floor. The professor said "What are you doing, the cup is full, stop pouring the tea!" As the master stopped pouring he said, *"Just the same as the cup is full, so is your mind. You came here to gain more knowledge from me; however, all you have done is tell me everything you already know. Empty your cup so that you may learn from others."*

This concept seems very simple, just like plain common sense, but it continues to amaze me how many people call me for advice and then argue with the information I share with them. While it is true that only you can build your business and change your life, but using the guidance and information of others who are where you wish to be, you can certainly escape many pitfalls and mistakes and get where you want to be more quickly. But you must accept that information and guidance and then put it into practice.

THE KEYS TO YOUR SUCCESS

It is the true nature of man to strive for success. More precisely, to strive to succeed, for it is not the accomplishment that is fulfilling it is the process. It's the journey, not the destination! And no matter what we do, that success is what we do for ourselves.

We are success driven creatures, why do you think so many people hate their jobs? There is nothing to accomplish no sense of reaching a new goal. However, I must say I believe this is often our own faults. We get lazy, we'd rather just have someone tell us what to do and get paid than to have to really try to accomplish anything. But then we slowly begin to hate our boss, our lives, and ourselves. And all along the one getting rich and accomplishing all their goals is the guy who owns the company we work for! And he got us to help him do it. Because of our laziness we've allowed ourselves to be used, our resources taped for someone else's gain!

Now you are probably asking yourself *"What does all this rambling have to do with making money?"* **EVERYTHING!!!** You must understand this one key before you will ever get anywhere, OZ NEVER GIVE NOTHING TO THE TIN MAN, THAT HE DIDN'T ALREADY HAVE!!! Confused? It's simple; you have everything you need to have the life you want inside you right now you only must believe it and begin your journey. Most of us live our lives in a complete daze, wandering from place to place too consumed by our day to day rituals to notice our lives are passing us by. John Lennon wrote "LIFE IS WHAT HAPPENS WHEN YOU'RE BUSY MAKING OTHER PLANS".

I don't believe any truer words have ever been spoken.

My point to all this here is that you must take responsibility for your own life, your journey to success and your journey to financial gain. You must find your own moneymaking machine, I'll help you all I can but until you understand that you must be "the prime source" you'll never fulfill your dreams. You can use my "model" as well you should and the model of any successful person, this is also key, to capitalize on the work of others, but in the end you must take the torch yourself.

If you want to learn more along these lines I highly suggest you read **THINK AND GROW RICH** by Napoleon Hill and **PSYCHO CYBER-NETICS** by Maxwell Maltz.

DO YOUR HOMEWORK

My mom used to tell me all the time "DO YOUR HOMEWORK!" Never did. At least not in school. But, I did figure out when I started in mail order that the best way to succeed was to find others who were succeeding and study what they were doing. Success leaves clues but…you have to seek out those clues.

I got some old money making magazines 2 and 3 years old and I compared the ads running in those with the ads that were running now. Most people were gone. So they failed. Some were still there. Same ad, everything. So obviously they were making money. A few had even expanded to bigger ads. They were really making money. I sent for the plans of all these advertisers. I studied their ads, the sales letters, the programs. I really studied what they were doing to find out what had made them successful. Why had these people made money and others had gone by the wayside.

After I ordered their programs, I either called them or wrote them with questions. Some were really nice and helpful and really took the time to answer my questions. Other folks, well, let's just say they didn't. I was able to build friendships with a select few of these people and to this day, they are still a source of support, guidance and friendship.

My point here is that if I had never investigated these companies, *done the homework*, I would have never met any other successful dealers and most certainly I would've never had the success I've had. I *pursued* my goal. I found others who were successful and picked their brains. I accepted what I learned and coupled their advice with my own trial and error and I made it happen.

And now I am here to share my knowledge with you, as it should be. And I'm still a student as well. We are all students and teachers at the same time. We have a responsibility to share what we have, the gift we've been given. I know it sounds a bit esoteric, but it's the way the universe works. It's all a big cycle. We really don't *own* anything¾we just borrow it for a while.

Chapter Two

The Secret

THE GOLDEN SECRET OF MAIL ORDER...THE REAL TRUTH BEHIND MONEY MAKING OFFERS!

What is the true secret behind every get-rich-quick, moneymaking offer that you have ever seen?

The true secret is:

It's not what you sell, it's how and where you sell it!

Simply put, it means that what is actually making the money is the advertisement or offer selling the product, not the product or secret plan itself.

There are two parts to these moneymaking offers.

1) The offer that entices you to send money for some new fantastic, secret moneymaker.

AND

2) The product or item they send to the people who buy the offer, usually a report, book or instruction manual.

Number two, the product, does not make the money, Number one, the offer, is the trigger that gets people to send their money.

Moneymaking offers have the ability to generate large amounts of cash very quickly. One successful advertisement or offer in one magazine can make a person rich in weeks or even days. A successful ad is one that gets people to send money, not necessarily the ad that offers the best product.

For example, let's say there are three ads/offers in a magazine. One is selling a horse race betting guide, the second is selling information on buying and selling government Jeeps, and the third offer is selling an instruction manual for selling books mail order.

Which offer do you think will be the most successful?

The answer is–NONE OF THEM!

No one sends money to get a horse betting manual or a guide to selling Jeeps. People do not want to bet on horses and they don't want to sell government Jeeps…

THEY WANT TO MAKE MONEY

The one that sells the best will be the one that has the most fantastic and motivational offer. You could be selling soap and if you convince people that they can get rich using your secret plan (for selling soap), then people will buy it.

When a person reads a moneymaking offer, they envision a special new secret or fantastic new miracle package that will make them money like magic. A wonderful secret that some rich guy is willing to share with anyone who will send $19.95, because he feels obligated to help others get rich, too.

What they are actually seeing is an advertisement designed to generate large amounts of cash in a short period of time. The only one who gets rich is the rich guy who made the offer.

There are no magic moneymakers.

All the money is earned from selling a product or service. When you work for a company, you are selling your time and skills to that company.

- A plumber sells his knowledge of drains when he comes to your house to clear a clog.
- A lawyer is selling his years of education and training when he collects payment from a client.
- A banker sells money to you when you go for a loan; you borrow a set amount and agree to pay back a fee above and beyond that amount in the form of interest.
- Horse racing tracks sell a chance to win even more money when people place bets on racehorses.

Horse racing tracks sell a chance to win even more money when people place bets on racehorses.

To make money you have to be selling something that people are buying. There are no magic tricks that will make money all by themselves and no secrets that will make you money for doing nothing. If there were, you wouldn't see people selling it in magazines.

ABOUT MONEYMAKING OFFERS

Is there any truth at all to these get-rich-quick programs? The answer is YES and NO.

There is truth to their claims of outrageous incomes. The problem is that what these offers tell you to do is not the real moneymaking formula. They are making a fortune selling secret plans that claim you can get rich following their simple instructions on how to:

BUY AND SELL EUROPEAN CARS

SELL BOOKS THROUGH THE MAIL

SHOW PEOPLE HOW TO PAY OFF THEIR MORTGAGES EARLY

BUY BONDS

BUY REAL ESTATE WITH NOTHING DOWN

SELL SPECIAL PACKAGES

BET ON HORSES AND WIN

The list goes on and on. There are too many of these offers to list. What is important to know is that they all share something in common?

WHAT DO THEY ALL HAVE IN COMMON?

All of these offers have some fantastic new plan or secret that will make you rich fast. And the people who know the secret are willing to share it with you, **if** you will send them money. They all have different ways to get you to send them money for their secret plan that will make you rich. They have all sorts of different gimmicks. Like selling government Jeeps or telling people how to erase bad credit.

If they already have a simple, easy plan to make money, why are they spending their time sending you offers through the mail? Why are they spending from one hundred to fifty thousand dollars to design and place advertisements in magazines and newspapers?

You have probably asked yourself while reading one of these offers–**"If this is really that easy and that profitable, why aren't they doing it?"** or **"Why would they be wasting their time sending me these letters or placing these ads, if they really had a fool-proof plan to get-rich-quick?"**

Smart marketing people know that you will be thinking this when you read their offer, so they put things like: **"I got so rich using my money-making plan that I can no longer keep it a secret and must share it with people."** or **"I have already made all the money I will ever need using my plan and now I feel compelled to help others make their fortunes."**

Don't believe it! These people are in this for the money! Lots of money!

One popular and profitable moneymaking offer instructs people to send for a fantastic moneymaking secret that can make you outrageous fortunes overnight. The people who answer their offers are sent a book. The book describes how to sell books and information through the mail. Not once in their full-page advertisement did they mention that what they were selling is a book on how to start your own business selling books through the mail. Yet that's what you received from them.

In their offer, they refer to what you are going to receive as **"a secret"**, **"our plan"**, or **"special material"**.

The question is: Why didn't they tell you in their offer that they were selling a book on how to start your own mail order business? After all, the book they send to you teaches you how to get fabulously wealthy selling books through the mail. Books on subjects like home gardening, sports strategies, health, etc. So, why is there no mention of a book in their offers?

Their moneymaking offer makes claims that you can earn outrageous fortunes overnight. Once you get their product it tells you the way to do it is to sell books through the mail.

So why not simply advertise the book? Why not tell people you can show them how to get rich selling books?

Their advertisement brings to mind some new and special secret that will make you rich. Some special process or trick that will make you rich overnight. It doesn't bring to mind selling books through the mail.

Why not? What kind of offer do you think people are more apt to buy?

1) An advertisement offering unlimited earning potential with very little investment using a secret plan or materials.

-OR-

2) An advertisement offering a book on "How to start your own business selling books through the mail."

Most people would answer the first advertisement of course. Everyone wants to have their own low investment, high profit business. They are enchanted by the opportunity to cash in on some new miracle, money-making formula.

On the other hand, many people don't want to buy and read another book, nor do they want to attempt to sell books through the mail.

You are probably not going to get rich overnight selling a book on gardening at home. But it *is* possible that one in a hundred or one in a thousand might be a success. It could happen, and that is how these offers can get away with making such fantastic claims. The Federal Trade Commission would not allow them to blatantly lie.

But if there is a chance that you could make a fortune selling government Jeeps or gardening books, then it is legal. Unfortunately, many people end up wasting valuable time and money on dead-end money schemes.

IT IS NOT WHAT THE PRODUCT TELLS YOU TO DO THAT MAKES FORTUNES. PEOPLE ARE NOT GETTING RICH SELLING GOVERNMENT JEEPS OR ERASING BAD CREDIT. THE PART THAT MAKES FORTUNES IS THE OFFER THAT SELLS THE PRODUCT!

A TYPICAL MONEYMAKING OFFER BROKEN DOWN

Imagine yourself reading a national magazine and you come across the advertisement (see enclosed) that I have placed in it. You answer my ad, sending me your check for $19.00, which you have post-dated thirty days in advance. In turn I send you my "secret plan" which turns out to be a book.

My book can be about anything from reducing mortgages to selling gardening books. But for this example, my book tells you how to sell good luck widgets through the mail. You can either make and sell your own "good luck widget" or buy "good luck widgets" from me.

My book explains how to set up your own office, get a business license, place advertisements, maintain a good mental attitude and a few other common business tips. But, in a nutshell, my book instructs you that the way to make your millions is to take out space advertisements and classified ads in magazines and newspapers to sell the "good luck widget".

I have delivered my end of the bargain. It is possible for someone to make a fortune selling good luck widgets, if they are incredibly lucky and come up with some fantastic way of marketing them. But, chances are, no one is going to get rich selling a widget.

You think it over. Although the book I have sent you does a good job of motivating you and gives you some important basics on starting and running your own business, you are skeptical about putting a lot of time, effort and money into selling widgets. So, you decide selling good luck widgets is not for you. You feel like you simply do not have enough faith in widgets or the courage or ability to make a go of selling them.

You actually have not given the plan an honest try. Therefore you do not take advantage of the money-back guarantee I have offered you. Or, you plan to return my book for a refund but you just don't seem to get around to finding a box, wrapping it up and writing a letter to return it. Before you know it the thirty days are over and you are stuck with my "secret plan".

Does this sound familiar? Millions of people go through this every year. Whether my plan tells you to sell books, European cars, government Jeeps or credit secrets, the results are often the same. You get a plan that could make a lot of money, but most reasonable people will not risk attempting them.

Remember:

IT'S NOT WHAT YOU SELL; IT'S HOW YOU SELL IT!!

The simple truth is that it is not the horse race betting or buying and selling Jeeps that makes fantastic amounts of money. It is the *offer* that got you to send me the $19.00 that makes incredible amounts of money.

You can have the best product in the world, but if you do not market it properly, it will fail. Likewise, if you have a relatively mediocre product with fantastic marketing it could make you a fortune.

The people who place these offers in magazines, newspapers and direct mailers are not doing it for charitable purposes. They are doing it for the money. Big money!

Just how much money are these offers capable of generating?

See for yourself. Go to your local library and ask for the current issue of the Standard Rate and Data book or SRDS. Look in the Opportunity seekers section. Notice all of the lists available for "income opportunity" products. Carefully look at the lists and find a few that are comprised of people who purchased an income opportunity book or a book on starting a business.

How many names are on those lists? 30,000, 150,000, 450,000? Each name represents a sale. A company, like the one in our example that sold a book on how to make a fortune overnight selling good luck widgets, sold income opportunity books to that many people.

What was the average unit of sale, i.e., how much do people pay for the book? Multiply the number of names on the list for the cost of the book and you have the amount generated by just one company.

This is proof of the fortunes that can be made and are being made.

Do several more of these companies and then compare. You can see the motivation behind these offers really is—HUGE PROFITS.

Now you know why these people are so willing to sell their moneymaking secrets. All it takes is one successful advertisement and you can have a small fortune in a short time.

How do *YOU* get your piece of this multi-billion dollar market?

If you want to realize the kind of fantastic earnings described in these offers.

Chapter Three

How To Make It Work

HOW TO MAKE YOUR FORTUNE
IN MAIL ORDER
GETTING TO THE POINT

The primary use of this system is to take advantage of the "key element" invariably hidden from the reader's level of awareness in all wealth building advertising. The use of the word "all" is applied confidently here because 100% of the successful money making advertising relies on a "Slight of hand" trick designed to part the reader from his money.

The "key element" hidden from the reader may seem simple and basic, but it is used lavishly by every major wealth building advertiser in nearly all national magazines; yet, the majority of us are simply blind to it. Many of these advertisers long ago became multi-millionaires because this element has been honed to such a fine degree. The reader's attention is deliberately diverted from the real money making opportunity, which is designed to earn a larger income for the promoter than for the buyer.

So much for the mystery! Now, just what is this hidden "key element?" Would you believe that it is the advertising itself?

CLEARING THE AIR

Okay, there is no "secrecy" regarding advertising. Everyone who has a need to sell something uses it. Advertising as a medium is old and well established, so this is certainly nothing new. However, especially as it applies to wealth building programs promoted through the use of national magazines, on down the line to include direct mail, attention is consciously directed away from the sales medium itself. The reader is led to concentrate on the "plan" or book, or whatever that is for sale. The natural conclusion by the reader is that the "plan" or book is what will develop a large amount of money by using the techniques expounded therein. The chances are, nothing could be further from the truth. Although some money may be made, it could most likely never equal that which the promoter brings in through the advertising he uses to sell it.

Besides being illogical for the advertiser to produce anything for someone else that will make more money than he is, the advertiser, knowingly or unknowingly, would not likely admit that his primary goal is just one thing; to get someone to buy his product, whatever that may be. If no one buys, he obviously isn't getting anywhere, in which case his "plan" or book would be of no value to anyone but himself–if even that. He therefore uses advertising as a means by which to make his sale, but there is a "fine line" distinction to be made here, especially as it applies to moneymaking plans.

In the first place, most moneymaking plans are, at best, only moderately successful for the majority of buyers, and it stands to reason why this would be so. Although the money making techniques may be proven or even ingenious, the buyer is not likely to be as psychologically or financially equipped as the promoter in making use of these techniques for himself. Perhaps the requirement for success is to "move mountains" or to have several thousand dollars available in order to make the techniques work. The promoter knows in advance that perhaps only 1 in 10 buyers will actually be able to earn anywhere near what either he himself has earned or what he projects the buyer can earn.

In the second place, the advertiser may already know that even he could not make money using his own promoted techniques. That would not be his main concern. However, because from his point of view there will be a large number of buyers who will neither try the techniques nor even ask for a refund, he is home free. In the meantime, he has made tons of money from his advertising alone.

This may seem to be a conspiracy of sorts, but it is more of a case of being the "Artful Dodger." The advertising has been used as a means to sell, but the product is the decoy. Enormous fortunes are continually being made by those who have recognized the difference between what they are selling versus getting people to buy it. It may be nothing more than outright "flimflam", for which reason most of us have been victims at one time or another. By purchasing many of these plans I often have become the "willing victim" in order to find out that the real money maker was the promoter's advertising.

When I finally learned this, I nearly fainted. Most people like me think, sure, the promoters are bound to make money, and that is the point. They do! And that is the new position I took, and the position you should be in, because the minute you recognize that you must be the advertiser, you will begin to make money.

Most buyers of wealth plans do not think of advertising anything of their own, since they assume that the "plan" is going to provide the means by which to make money. In fact, even if the "plan" includes prepared advertising, most people don't even consider the aspect of advertising itself as the principle means by which to make a fortune. Yet, the "key element" in making large sums of money is not necessarily to develop an amazing book or product, or using already prepared advertising. But to attract–on your own–many thousands of buyers by use of a "knock 'em dead" ad, then to provide something to justify the ad in the first place.

This is where my system comes in, because my intent is to provide you the means of putting into action these techniques being used by very successful advertisers which will, for a change, put money in the bank for you. Now that we have the "dirty laundry" out of the way, we can concentrate on the method of doing this. If you keep in mind that the number one goal is to produce a sale, the rest will follow in easy fashion. I have put together a three-step method, which will bring you money 100% of the time you use it.

Before I proceed, for those of you who think there is deception under-foot here, I would like to put your conscience at ease. Neither you nor I will be using this system as a means to cheat anyone. The opposite is true, because this system works 100% of the time–if done properly–and will earn you money. As shown later on as I get into the discussion of it, you will see that as you apply these techniques, your buyers will get the same benefits as you. In other words, everyone wins. Using this cor-rectly can and will provide you and everyone who learns of it, a fabu-lous income. As long as there are "mail order" enthusiasts and the national media at your disposal, you will never lack for buyers.

I also want to cover various aspects of the advertising industry so that, regardless of your budget (which must be small if you are still looking for a way to develop wealth), you won't go to the poor house by spend-ing more than you can afford in order to get the results you need.

SECRET OF WEALTH

About now, you are probably wondering what makes this system so different. The answer is that hardly anyone uses it, and those who do are very rich, indeed! Let's get a little more background.

Chain letters and MLM make up the bulk of the opportunities advertised in the nation's hundreds of independent publications or by direct mail dealers. By contrast, these same offers are not visibly apparent in national advertising seen in major publications such as Income Opportunities or Entrepreneur. There are at least two important reasons for this: one, the expense would be prohibitive. And two, the publisher's editorial department would not allow them to appear.

If what you are receiving in your mailbox is an indication of all the moneymaking activity going on, business clearly is thriving. So what we are looking at is a massive "underground" attempt to develop wealth by mostly unorthodox means. This has resulted in enticing ads for wealth building, which have become more prevalent than in recent memory and even more blatant. This is "prime time" for snake oil salesmanship. The competition is tough as more and more clever salesmen peddle their wares. And this is where they lead the unwary astray.

Snake oil salesmen rely on the development in our country that we're a nation of consumers. We have a choice of ten of everything. This suggests that the more we have of something the more flexible the market will be, and the more buyers there will be for something new and catchy. Whether this is true or not, we have constantly pounded into our heads that we need products because the flaw in the product line of sales is the fact that we are simply glutted by "new" and "catchy" items. Which is not to say that they are not good. However, the profit factor enjoyed by the manufactures bear little relationship to what the individual who takes up selling them will earn.

Now look at those rare persons who have seen through this flaw and who are the ones to catch the big fish. You know who they are by their big, full-page ads in national magazines. Understanding the frustrations experienced by others–because they have experienced them themselves–they have come to concentrate on developing wealth-building concepts of their own both workable and unworkable. Their ideas are enunciated in the books they write followed by "back end" sales of additional information they may develop as they go along. Further money is made by selling your name to mailing list companies so that you can receive even more offers.

As mentioned earlier, this entire game plan is well calculated and is a proven way to do business and is also a great moneymaker. Not necessarily for you, but for them. The advertiser has put to use a great psychological ploy, because he knows that, being product oriented, buyers will come out of the woodwork in order to discover how to sell the new and wondrous! The failure rate is high because in search of independence, the majority of these people get bogged down in putting these often time impossible ideas to work.

Clearly, then, the reason most people don't make much money in mail order is because they don't initiate plans of their own. If a person does not have complete control of what is going on out there, or is at the mercy of an unethical promoter, he can't expect to set the world on fire.

This system unlocks the secret door, so that some light can shine in. It consists of important elements which have become apparent to those who have become successful as a sure way to become rich. These are:

    1. Be your own boss; initiate your own program

2. Be in complete control of what you do
3. Develop your own advertising
4. Don't give up

Writing a successful, moneymaking ad can be simple. Just a little on, I will get into detail on how to develop an ad that is used only by wealth-building millionaires. In any case, I am sure that you will find that ad writing will be a terrific ego trip, because not only will thousands-even millions-of people be reading your words, you can experience the great thrill of being paid for them.

This system reviewed up to this point is avoiding moneymaking losers. Which ones are these? The ones you are losing money on! If it has to do with products or dependence upon other people, the chances are that all your efforts are going to waste. This system is, above all, advertising. You will have noticed by now, I hope, that advertising in this instance is more important than the item that is for sale. This is because what is being sold is secondary to getting the sale. Now you should understand why you may have been disappointed in programs you have purchased in the past.

You see, in most instances of individuals placing national, full-page ads for their moneymaking programs, the item for sale more than likely merely justifies the ad. Only a relative handful of people in this country know that, and none of these advertisers would willingly admit that for at least one obvious reason. They strive to meet legal requirements in selling information by mail. A book, no matter how bizarre-so long as it is not obscene-can legally meet postal requirements. This is the only criterion they need to pay attention to. If you can't succeed using their techniques, the problem, they may claim, is not theirs but yours. Some advertisers have a greater sense of ethics than others do and this is reflected by the value of information received. This success system being only a term has no conscience and does not describe a degree of ethics. It only shows that it works.

So, the fact is, advertising-especially particularly designed advertising-works, 100% of the time. Additional "secret" knowledge, which we will go into, can be applied in producing an absolutely huge amount of money every time you use it, then putting together an ad that draws thousands upon thousands of responses, and you will have a money-maker for life.

Now that we have looked at being boss, initiating your "own" program and the advertising, perhaps the fourth element is the most important, and that is:

KEEP AT IT

Tenacity. What a word! As applied in the here it means just plain not giving up. The stakes are just too high! Almost all great successes are built upon the ruins of earlier failures, and you can be sure that one wealth-building advertiser after another learned from their errors. I intend to lead you around those errors, so that you will experience as few as possible. By contrast, spending a great deal of time and energy on losing projects which are slow moving, produce few rewards and give you little or no control, will only rob you of your vitality and inner drive.

As used here, tenacity can reap excellent rewards quickly because, you can concentrate on a single effort, which is writing your own advertising copy. This is all you have to do for now. Interestingly, it has been shown many times that an effort that is totally focused on just one thing produces astonishing results. What happens is that the mind locks out distractions and sends out strict orders to the body to conform to your will. Once you realize that you truly wish to accomplish something, the mind will be your partner instead of a negative influence. In fact, the mind-as opposed to the will-can produce a fascinating display of talent you never thought you had.

For all of us the mind often wants to behave like an unbridled horse, first taking one path then another without any great sense of direction. Worse, the mind really dislikes discipline and is a frequent complainer. Like a cranky neighbor, when displeased, it sends a message to the body telling it to develop a headache or tiredness-anything to keep the will from over powering it. But convince it that you have found a way to become very rich and that you need its cooperation, it will suddenly behave like an actor waiting in the wings, ready to supply you with all the materials necessary for writing the best ad copy you ever saw.

The reason why you must take control of your mind by not allowing it to drift from the goal is because money-making advertising commonly seen in national publications are not the same as manufactures use in selling soap or toothpaste. In contrast to any other kind of advertising, wealth-building ads are almost always completely centered upon the advertiser. Before a word is written on a solution to poverty, we are treated to a very personal account of the writer's past. If you haven't seen these ads already, buy a copy of Income Opportunities magazine and look these ads over carefully. If you haven't shed at least a few tears, you have missed something!

This is why you need "all of you". No one can be convincing regarding whom he is what he is or why he is appealing for your money unless he knows. You need your mind to look down deep inside yourself to find these things out for yourself. Who knows? You might be surprised! Once you learn this, and it may not be easy, then the words will have meaning because they originated from your deepest self. You see, false sentiments or shallow self-related stories smell to high heaven. National advertising is expensive, and it is a highly developed medium by which to put millions of dollars into your bank account instead of nickels. There is then little room for error.

The rewards to "knowing yourself"–even if you never earn a dime are also great, because when you are sure of yourself and what you really want out of this world, you never again will have problems with concentration, making your mind do exactly as you wish, focusing on the goals you want, or losing interest halfway down the track. You will be tenacious as a bird dog absolutely determined to keep the scent, so as to ultimately find its quarry.

Tenacity also is very much tied in with the controlling aspect of this system. It simply must be there. In the past, you may have lost the desire to succeed because the path is so littered with obstacles. Most likely, however, you never had control but were at the mercy of a "company" or some other entity. This factor causes endless grief and loss of vital spirit which you need to sustain. If at anytime you feel that you are working for someone else, I suggest that you are doing it wrong.

I hope you can see that by applying its principles you become much more the individual than you perhaps ever were before. Furthermore, you don't merely write your ad, you are the ad. That's right. Your personality is right out there for everyone to see. There are limits to this vulnerability, of course, which we will examine, but when you do this well and are convincing, you may not get the "Oscar" for best performance, but you darned well will be richer than before.

THE AD

We should define the kind of ad that is necessary to develop the high level of income we are looking for. It must be full-page size with a coupon. There are no substitutes. Classified advertising is an entirely different realm, which we will look at later on.

The idea of "copy writing" may be a total turnoff to people who get nervous writing even the shortest of letters only once a year, and then only when absolutely necessary. People, who can talk half a day on most any subject, freeze up at the mere idea of putting thought to paper. This may be due to bad memories of school days. The difference from those days to now maybe that there is no crotchety teacher standing over you watching you sweat. There are no "exams" to dread, or papers to turn in. There is only you working out in the language you are used to what it is you want the reader to see. No more, no less. It might even amaze you that if you are not used to writing, your struggles will add to the genuine feeling you want to convey.

This is not to say that your ad should bear the mark of a beginner, only that the real you comes across in your work. I suggest starting by using the accepted format commonly used in wealth building ads seen in national publications. You can hurry to the store and buy several issues if you want, but before you go, write your own first using the format I will give you. This way, your original thoughts will stay intact. You may have to change them as you go, and probably you will end up rewriting five or six times, shortening, lengthening or whatever, to make it sound right. Don't worry about spelling, grammar or sentence structure at this point. You can fool with those later. The idea is to say what you want as easily as possible.

HEADLINE

First of all, write the headline of the ad. This is probably the most important part of the entire ad, because this is where the reader's eye must stop. You don't want him to turn the page to go on to something else. Whatever the headline is, it must lead to the subcaption, which is the sentence directly below the headline and above the body of the ad.

Now that we have those two critical elements, let's look at them. For the headline: Be fresh and original. How to do this? Don't look at other wealth-building ads until you have explored your own mind and have written down what you think you should write. Headlines are usually very short, but long enough to snap the reader to attention. Use "key" words, which will help you, do this, such as: "At last"…"New"…"Revolutionary"…"Now"…"How to"…

If these key words are not comfortable for you, don't use them. It is better to be original than stilted.

However, you can make use of certain words fairly easily when you are sure of the thought you want to convey. If you want to explain your position, you can use the word "why". You can make a promise, such as, "I promise that," and then follow it up with a method that will be quick and easy. I would avoid the word "amazing" due to its over use. You can live without it.

There are dozens of ways of getting to the same theme and your way may be more successful than mine. Never assume that there is a perfect headline or even ad copy. The best headline and ad copy are what produce sales, and you won't know this until you've tried it.

SUBCAPTION

Now, for the subcaption. This can be one or two sentences, and very little more, which further develop the thought conveyed in the headline. Here you can use "why", "how to", or any key words you didn't use in the headline. Don't repeat yourself. Just follow through with the subject. Don't explain anything at this point, because you want the reader's eye to naturally drop down to the ad copy, where you will do all your explaining. Nevertheless, the subcaption must continue to hold the reader's interest, otherwise he won't read any further. There must be some mystery involved here so that he will look into your ad copy to find the answer.

BODY COPY

Should you make it long or short? That depends on you and how long it takes you to say what you want, but always keep it to one page. You can do 1,500 words in typesetting and still not need a microscope to read it. You can say a lot in 1,500 words and still have a single page. A single page, incidentally, makes economic sense wherever you advertise.

First paragraph: Next in importance to the headline and the subcaption, this is where you don't want to lose your reader. It is here you must tell what you will do for him-but not how. The mystery continues. Whatever flair you have for writing, use it here and your personal story that follows. Don't be cute or clever, because this is strictly business. Write this paragraph several or even a dozen times, put it aside for a while, then come back to it. This is the "gut feeling" time, although it may not look like it when you are done. Perhaps every desire of wealth and experience of anguish you have ever felt should be apparent at this time. Dig into yourself and get emotional. What you come up with may be brilliant.

Second Paragraph: This may lead on to the Third Paragraph. Before you spend time explaining what your plan is (which may be this one); you must tell the reader what it isn't. This should be easy, since you have been exposed to this secret. Yet, you can't list a dozen items. Two or three will do, and later on more can be worked in. The reader should now be curious, especially if he learns that this plan will be easy and inexpensive.

Fourth Paragraph: In this paragraph and subsequent paragraphs you can now begin telling your own story. How you searched for and found the answer to prosperity, and how this discovery will surely do the same for the reader. Names of friends or people you know who have tried it and succeeded with it will add much credibility. Your personal story can go on at length, if you wish. You can open the door to your life, but you don't have to tell it all. Then begin hitting hard at being convincing, showing that this plan will work for the reader. Please remember that this plan is for his benefit, not yours. You have already succeeded and the reader should be keenly envious. He should want to achieve as much as you, if you have made it easy and attractive for him.

Toward the end of the copy, and after assuring him that the offer is limited, it's time to talk money. Now is the time to tell how much this will cost him. After you have explained so thoroughly how much he can make using your plan, he should be surprised that it is so inexpensive- and it is! He isn't aware that wealth-building plans advertised nationally are priced from $20 to $40 in order to be competitive. $40 is really excessive, while $25 to $30 are currently most common. Emphasize more than once that the price is reasonable, and it is!

Finally, we get to the real sales pitch, although you have been "selling" all along. This is where the reader learns how much he will get for so little and how strongly you feel that he can do nothing but gain by buying this plan.

Here is where the faint-hearted advertiser pauses, because he knows that if he doesn't add a guarantee he will lose the opportunity for the sale. That horrible word "refund" must appear, and if he is honest, must be prepared to provide it.

Now that we are prepared to accept postdated checks, and have shown that our guarantee will be good for 30 days, it is time to get the sale-for sure! If you don't ask for the sale, you probably won't get it. Asking doesn't mean begging by saying, "Please buy…" Asking can be, "So why not see for yourself that…" or "Let me prove to you that…" Do not demand except in an inoffensive way, such as, "Buy now and you will see that…" You can lead the reader into action, such as, "Don't wait another minute…" You can give and take away; one minute it's available and next it's almost gone. You can offer a choice, such as between poverty or wealth. You can bring him into the picture by allowing him to imagine what it must feel like to be rich. (It's very nice!)

A further opportunity for the "sale" is in the coupon, which follows. It must stick to the point but affirm the reader's decision to buy. That means RUSH the information. Assume he wants it NOW. Offer same-day-as-received shipment. Otherwise he may worry that it may take weeks to arrive. If he thinks that, he will forget it and go on to the next offer.

NOTE: The limited offer will be limited in its availability if only because it will evolve over time. What you offer now you may not in the future. This is certainly how I perceive this system. Advertising changes, resulting in different offers. You may give away more now than later, or the price will go up. In the meantime, the reader must feel that if he doesn't buy now he will lose the opportunity of a lifetime. You can mention this one or more times in the ad copy, but not necessarily in those words. It is a much-overused phrase.

Most of all these techniques are used daily in wealth-building advertising. They pay and pay and pay. Now that you know them, you will be wiser than before when such a wealth-building salesman tries to "lay a number" on you. When these techniques are used in a subtle manner, they are rarely noticed. The reader gets totally carried away with the message-and the desire to become rich. That desire should-if you have painted a beautiful picture for him-give you the sale. Fortunately this is true, because this information is not generally available in this context, as moneymaking ads (shown here) are unique and not the least big orthodox.

Now that you have an idea of how all this is put together, try it yourself. Do it over and over until you feel that, WOW!, you wouldn't hesitate for a moment to buy the program you have. Now compare your ad with those appearing in such national magazines as Income Opportunities or Entrepreneur. YOUR EYES WILL BE OPENED–no doubt, once and for all! Now you can "fine tune" your own ad without becoming confused. You can also start calculating your new income because all that you have learned so far has helped to lift the veil of secrecy which has kept you from enjoying a lifetime of wealth.

IMPORTANT! Consider the appearance of these ads and the ad to which you responded. Notice that few, if any, frills exist except for photo inserts. The rest is strictly business, which means no artwork borders or decoration of any kind. Emphasis is on eye-stopping headlines, strong subcaptions, tear-jerking ad copy, coupled with astounding solutions of financial miseries, followed by giveaway price and unconditional guarantee. With all this, who needs "doo-dads" cluttering a thoroughly structured and already proven method?

When your ad is ready, have it typeset so that the paste up can accommodate changes, proofread it yourself at least twice for errors. You want flawless copy, as "typos" will glare out at you every time you look at your ad in a publication: others will see it as a "hatchet job", and not be inclined to buy. You will have already checked your spelling and grammar to be sure that those are right. If you are in doubt put the printer on alert, and most will happily pre-check the copy with you before they get going on it. Helvetica type in 8-pt size will allow you approximately 3,400 words, and that is with using a photo insert and a 20-point bold headline and 14-point subcaption. Keep your "master" in perfect condition and use it to make the "camera-ready" copies, unfolded, you will need to send to the publication in which they will appear.

The media is next on our agenda. If you have been petrified up to this point about how much all this will cost you, my advice is to relax. While major national publications charge an arm and a leg for single full-page ad (which shouldn't surprise you), we will look at the alternative. Believe me, you will be impressed to learn that working with even the lowest of budgets, nearly anyone can afford to advertise as needed and still get astonishing results.

Chapter Four

Nuts And Bolts

THE MEDIA

There is a difference in the kind of advertising you can depend on. All advertising needs to be tested for its salability. To spend even $500 to start only to be disappointed can be devastating to your self-esteem, your inner drive, and your budget. Since you may already be an "old timer" in mail order, such advertising may never have entered your mind. Possibly this is because so many wealth programs seen in the "underground" publications almost always encourage the use of direct mail and the classified.

THE CLASSIFIED

If you have been active at all in mail order marketing, you may have already found a use for classified advertising in the many independent publications which specialize in this. Because the classified ads are the least expensive advertising available in any media, it is an obvious choice. A 20-word ad in a national publication, however, can easily cost $200 or more. Independent publications are far less, usually in the $20 or $25 range. Keeping in mind that a proper classified should not ask for money, since it is used only to develop leads, a "proper" response refers back to the direct mail "classic format" approach. Because this is rarely done in independent advertising responses, simply sending a copy of your full-page ad with cover letter will work well.

THE REAL WAY TO MAKE MONEY MAILING CIRCULARS FROM HOME

One method of mail order selling is drop shipping. With this method, you work on a commission basis and someone else produces the product and ships it to the customer.

The basic method of operation is this: You obtain circulars from a company or individual offering a particular product or service. You put your name and address on the circulars and mail them out to people who are likely prospects for the items offered. When someone wants to purchase an item, they must send the order and payment to you. You take out your commission and send the rest of the money and a shipping label addressed to your customer to the supplier. The supplier will then ship the item directly to your customer using your shipping label. The package the customer receives appears to come directly from you. This is known as "drop-shipping" because the responsibility for shipping the merchandise is "dropped" on the supplier.

The usual commission offered to mailers is 50 percent of the retail price, although higher commissions are sometimes offered.

There are a lot of good home mailing programs you can make money with. The best way to find out about them is to get copies of the various mail order trade magazines. There are hundreds of these publications. They are put out mainly by small publishers and mail order dealers. They consist mostly of ads promoting business plans, moneymaking ideas, commission mailing programs, etc. Look through some of these and answer those ads that interest you.

There are some programs that have both the benefits of commission mailing and selling your own item, but without some of the drawbacks. Some companies will offer a dealership program that allows you to keep all the money you receive and will ship the order to your customer for just the postage cost. These are called "All Profit Dealerships".

You may wonder why a company would do this and how they could make any money. The main reason it is done is to add names to their mailing lists. If someone buys a moneymaking type offer from you, then he has proven his interest in that kind of item. When your supplier fills the order, he will add the customer's name to his mailing list and send his other offers to him. He may also stuff some of his own offers in with the order itself. Of course, if the item you are selling is a dealership set-up to sell other items, the supplier is going to benefit from this as well. The more dealers he has helping him sell his items, the better. Both the mailer and the suppler benefit from this type of arrangement.

OPPORTUNITY SEEKERS

Selling information to people who are looking for ways to make more money is big business. People who are looking for business plans, moneymaking programs, and related information are know as Opportunity Seekers. There are 30 to 50 million of them at any given time, and they are interested in buying printed and recorded information, such as books, booklets, folios, reports, courses, audio cassettes and video tapes.

The best opportunity seekers to mail to are new ones. They haven't been over exposed to hundreds of different moneymaking offers or lost interest in starting their own business.

After a person answers a few ads, he will soon become flooded with offers. This reduces your chances of getting an order from him.

A lot of mailing activity goes on between mail order dealers, and you might be led to believe that dealers are just mailing to each other. Money can be made by mailing to other dealers, but the most money is made from fresh opportunity seekers.

All of this mailing activity that goes on between mail order dealers can be called the "Inner Circle of Mail Order". As you get deeper into this field you will receive more and more of these mailings. This material can be very useful to you. From it you will be able to pick up new orders to sell to opportunity seekers. You will also find quite a few advertising vehicles through which you can promote your offers. There are hundreds of trade magazines, tabloids, and small ad sheets that are distributed to an amazing number of home workers, opportunity seekers and mail order dealers. The ad rates are very low compared to the newsstand publications.

A package of offers and publications sent out by a mail order dealer to a prospect is commonly referred to as a "Big Mail". You will find lots of interesting material in a good big mail, such as: articles by experienced mail order dealers, trade publications, sources of low-cost typesetting, printing, rubber stamps, and advertising; dealership offers and other money-making opportunities.

Money can be made by mailing to inner circle dealers, but you'll get better response by mailing to fresh opportunity seekers. To reach these opportunity seekers, you use mailing lists, classified and display advertising, or a combination of both.

The mail order publications have smaller circulations than the newsstand magazines, but they are targeted directly to the most likely prospects for moneymaking offers. The newsstand publications have a more generalized readership with only a small percentage of readers looking for moneymaking offers. They are still good for your advertising though, because their circulations are so high, making this relatively small percentage of opportunity seekers really add up.

Mailing lists of opportunity seekers are another way to get your offers into the hands of good prospects. You can reach thousands of people within days by mailing to a list. The drawback is that it costs more than placing ads. You also need to be careful not to get stuck with a bad list. Many companies rent out mailing lists that are worthless and it's a waste of your money to mail to them. There are many factors that will determine the response of a mailing list to an offer. The freshness of the names is one. If the list is old, many of the people will no longer be interested in the type of item you are offering. Some of them will have moved or died. It is very important that mailing lists be constantly updated to compensate for these problems. Unresponsive names should be removed and replaced with new ones. Address corrections should be made.

Response will also be affected by whether the list is made up of inquiries or proven buyers. It is also essential that the people on the list be interested specifically in the type of item you are offering, or in something very similar.

The idea here is to target, out of the millions of people in this country, just the right type of consumer who is likely to be interested in what you have to offer, and has displayed this interest with action.

When renting a list, you should look for this information.

1. How old are the names on the list?
2. Are they inquiries, proven buyers, or both?
3. Is the list updated?

As you begin to receive response to your advertising you will build your own mailing list. People who have bought from you in the past are the best prospects for your future offers. Keep your list up to date by using the Post Office Address Correction Service. Simply print "ADDRESS CORRECTION REQUESTED" on the envelope (up to two ounces). If undeliverable, the piece will be returned to you with an explanation as to why it is undeliverable, plus the new address if it is known. There is a small fee for this service. Check with your local Postmaster for current cost.

What you must realize when mailing to a mailing list is that your response rate is going to be lower than if you were to mail to the same number of people who had responded to your classified or display advertising. People who respond to your ads are the best prospects because they have qualified themselves with action. They have proven their interest in your offer by taking the time to write to you to learn more. On the other hand, the people you send "cold mailings" to may not be interested in your offer at all, so you are possibly wasting postage and printed materials.

Placing ads is a good way to "weed out" those who aren't interested in your offers. Using mailing lists and print is more of a shotgun approach. You send your offer to a large number of people in the hope that a small percentage of them will respond to your offer and allow you to make back your expenses plus a profit. Both methods have their good and bad points. You will have to determine your own goals and the amount of money you can safely invest to achieve them.

Advertising is basically what the Mail Order Business is all about. You must project an image of professionalism with your sales literature. Don't skimp in this department. Use the highest quality printed materials you can. Remember: In Mail Order the customer will rarely, if ever, see you in person. The only thing they will see is what you mail to them. A prospect may be hesitant to order if your literature is sloppy or poorly printed.

Your small space display ads should always be professionally typeset. Most of the mail order typesetters are very inexpensive and it's well worth the small charge to have them set-up your ads.

You will find that a lot of the mail order dealership programs come with display ads that have blank spaces in which you insert your name and address. If it's a small ad, especially a one-inch or two-inch, avoid typing in your name and address. Never write it by hand. Instead use professionally typeset name and address strips. These are also available from mail order typesetters.

Another important thing to take care of is having a letterhead typeset. This doesn't have to be anything fancy or expensive. Something simple and dignified with your name, address, and a descriptive line of your business print in black ink on white paper will do nicely. Again, this can be done by a mail order typesetter, or local printer.

Always type your business correspondence. Most large companies will ignore handwritten letters. You don't appear to be a serious business person to them if you send them handwritten letters. It also doesn't look very professional to the customer if your letters are hand written. You must gain the confidence of your prospective customers, or you will not make many sales. Type your correspondence on a typeset letterhead. Use printed envelopes with your name and address typeset on them. This will give your letters a totally professional look which is so important in this business. Don't underestimate the importance of this.

Study and learn all you can about the mail order field. Add to your knowledge by reading books, booklets, folios, and other reports on the subject. You will also find it very useful to read books on advertising.

If you really want to be successful in mail order, you must be **persistent**. So many people quit when they don't get rich overnight. Even though mail order is very easy to get into, it is still a **business**, and must be treated as such. Don't give up too soon if things don't seem to be working out at first. When you place ads, you must realize that it usually takes a few consecutive insertions for an ad to produce results. Most people need to see an ad more than once before they will respond. If you only run an ad in a publication once, it probably won't produce much for you.

When the money starts coming in, re-invest it into your business. Put as much of it as you can back into more advertising. Advertising is the lifeblood of mail order; you can't make any money without it.

THE SECOND SECRET TO SUCCESS IN MAIL ORDER

Julian Simon, author of "HOW TO START AND OPERATE A MAIL ORDER BUSINESS", calls this secret "the professional method of finding products." Though he is mainly referring to products, the same rules apply to information reports.

Many non-mail order corporations and practically all successful mail order businesses use this secret, which is simply:

SUCCESSFULLY SELL WHAT IS ALREADY BEING SOLD

I'm not saying go and copy someone's report; civil and criminal penalties go along with such actions. Remember, the way words are expressed can be copyrighted, but you can't copyright ideas.

Observe the advertising of books and reports already on the market. If the ad has been running for months or even years, it is safe to conclude that it has been successful. Thus, it is also safe to assume that a similar report would do as well or hopefully even better.

Studying your competitor enables you to avoid areas of unnecessary failure. Your competitor has shown you that there is a market for this particular report and has also shown you which magazines to advertise in.

Analyzing his promotions will enable you to see the kinds of appeals he makes to his prospects and how involved he is with direct mail.

The type of marketing I'm going to show you is virtually risk-proof, starting with classifieds and small space ads. I'll have more on this later.

I have studied and analyzed many successful ads and procedures in the number of years I have been involved with mail order. This principal, the "copy-cat" method, is what I find to be the secret of success behind most mail order operations.

If you're like most beginners, you don't have the capital or experience to promote a new report successfully. You should choose a subject similar to one already being sold but one that is in a broad range of similarity.

This is not to say you shouldn't be original; in fact, be as original as you want, just don't be so far-fetched that you can't sell your idea.

THE SUCCESS SYSTEM

While there are many essentials necessary to profitably sell information by mail, the most important are:
1. The strength of your advertising
2. The right subject
3. The correct advertising method
4. The right idea
5. The price of your report
6. A quick and easy method must be offered
7. A basic need must be satisfied

The strength of your advertising. It doesn't matter whether you are using classifieds, space ads or direct mail—the advertising is the money maker! Good advertising can sell anything! This is the single most important factor of all.

The right subject. You already know that. It's information of how-to or self-help character and generally unavailable information appealing to a large audience. You are safer if you start selling something similar to what is already being sold.

The correct advertising method. There are three basic methods: one, selling straight from the ad whether classified or display; two, selling by direct mail, where you mail your offer to a list of names you purchase; and three, advertising for inquiries through classifieds and/or display ads, and mailing your sales literature to all who ask for it. For beginners with limited capital and experience, the only sensible method is the third method, advertising for inquiries and following up with sales literature.

The right media. Even if you do nothing else right, placing your ad in the wrong magazine will cause you to fail. If you are going to sell an opportunity or money making type report, you will benefit greatly from the list of best magazines in the advertising section. Otherwise, go "where the action is". Place your ad in media where your competitors are consistently selling their material.

The price of your report. It doesn't matter if you are selling the best report in print: if it isn't priced right you won't be in business long. Price it generally along the same scale as your competitors unless it is of an extremely high value–then test carefully. The best price is usually between $5 and $18 for a 45-150 page book of 8½" x 11" size. For a 70-150 page 5½" by 8½" sized book, prices usually run about $8 to $12, with $10 the most common price. Of course, testing at various prices will reveal the most profitable price at which you should sell. But ordinarily, if you charge less than $5, you're only swapping dollars.

Should offer a quick and easy method. Your report should, as much as possible, offer a relatively quick and easy (or inexpensive) method for achieving the benefits your prospects desire.

Must satisfy a basic need. The basic needs and desires the average normal person has are these:

a. Financial success - money and the things money will buy
b. Love in all its forms
c. Ego gratification - pride, dignity, recognition
d. Good health
e. Personal power
f. The opportunity for creative expression and new experiences
g. The need to belong - a sense of roots

In order for a normal person to be completely happy with life, all these needs and desires must be fulfilled. If just one is missing a person may find him/herself in a state of mild restlessness or in a state of extreme dissatisfaction with life.

Nothing will be able to stop you from being successful if you can show people how to fulfill just one of these needs and convince them that your report will help.

These seven essentials are the backbone of your business and neglecting them will result in disaster. Even if you do 100 other things wrong, you will still make money if you follow these essentials.

HOW LONG WILL IT TAKE TO MAKE MONEY

This is probably the most asked question I receive. The answer depends on a lot of factors, most of which come down to the person asking the question.

If you follow a proven system or method and do everything right, you should be able to make money in a very short amount to time. The key here is what you do with your first profit. Most folks believe they can take that first profit and begin spending it, which they can if they want to put their business in the ground very quickly.

But it is the wise ones that see the big picture and reinvest those profits back into the business to keep it rolling along and growing. So many folks are dead set on this get-rich quick mentality–the amount of people still participating in chain letters is proof enough of that. And that type of mindset is what is killing many would-be profitable operations.

Let's say you do your homework and start with one small classified ad that costs you $120. After all is said and done you end up with $200 total, that's an $80 profit. Now take your $80 profit and add another $40 and run two ads for $240. After both ads run you have a profit of $160 plus you have a list of say 200 people you send a 2nd mailing to. That turns maybe another $300 profit. So all together you've profited $540 in a couple months. If you keep this going expanding into 10 to 12 magazines and doing a 2nd mailing in just 8 to 12 months you could easily be bringing in over $1,000 a week–now is the time to start paying yourself and spending some of that money.

Now you can easily speed up this process either using a direct mail campaign or starting with more than one ad. But this example was just to show how someone could start with a small amount of money and slowly build a solid steady income. This is very realistic and very possible for anyone to do.

I hope I've convinced you to look at your business as a business and to work for the end result. I truly believe that anyone can build a steady income in mail order if they're simply willing to learn and apply proven, solid methods.

Chapter Five

Fine Tuning The Machine

HOW I GENERATE OVER 500 LEADS A WEEK FOR NEXT TO NOTHING

Here's the secret method that many others have paid up to $30 for. It's really very simple and you've probably already started doing it even though you don't know it...

Step 1: Write a short letter like this: "Dear Sirs–I am an opportunity seeker and I'm currently involved in Multi-Level Marketing. Please send me your price list for renting names ASAP! Thank you."

Step 2: Send out a letter like this to every mailing list advertiser you see in all the opportunity magazines out there.

Step 3: Go through all of the same magazines and answer *every* ad offering "free information" or a free report. Once they've sent you the information, these dealers will sell your name to other mailing list companies as well.

Step 4: Repeat this process every 60-90 days.

What happens is all the mailing list companies that you wrote to will put you on their list as well, so you'll start receiving tons of offers from people who rented your name. 99% of these people are new to mail order and MLM as you'll be able to tell when you receive tons of chain letters, very poorly copied and produced flyers, and multitudes of the same offer from different people. So what you have is a group of highly motivated (they rented a list and mailed to it!) but not very experienced opportunity seekers...now *that's* a hot list!

These people will bite on mailing list offers, money making programs, dealerships, and multi-level marketing programs. They are desperately trying to make money and if you just convince them that you can show them how or that your program will do it for them, you've got a goldmine on your hands!

Every chain letter contains 4-6 names and there's always numerous Multi-Level Marketing packages flying around. Once you're on all the big lists you'll easily be pulling in 500 names a week from this "junk" mail.

Plus you can collect the names in your computer and rent them out to other people. There is big money to be made doing this!

By repeating this process every 60-90 days, you insure that you're staying at the top of the lists so you're getting the freshest names available. You see, most of the companies that advertise in the opportunity magazines will keep your name on the list so long as it's deliverable, but you'll gradually make it down the list and won't get rented as often. You want to stay at the top. Most of the people sending you offers are *losing* money and will bite on nearly anything that sounds good. Mailing list offers work well with these folks and they've discovered the hard way that those cheap lists are no good.

THE ONE SECRET THAT INSTANTLY DOUBLED THE RESPONSE RATE TO MY MAILINGS

The one secret I stumbled upon that doubled the response rate to my mailings is this: An opportunity seeker is a broad term that can end up costing you a lot of money if you're not careful! To elaborate, I always bought "RED HOT OPPORTUNITY SEEKER LISTS" either from one of those companies in the opportunity magazines or from someone who sent me a sales letter in the mail. I had okay success, sometimes better than others.

Then one day, I read an article about matching your offer to your mailing list. The article talked about the fact that using a list of known mail order buyers is okay, but if you had say a catalogue selling home stereo equipment, you'd get a much better response with a list of known home stereo equipment buyers than just known mail order buyers. And if the list were known home stereo equipment buyers who purchased by mail, you'd get an even better response.

This got me to thinking and I did a little digging. I discovered that *most* of these big companies offering names in the opportunity magazines were buying these names from other people who were running ads in these same magazines. And *anyone* who shows interest in making money is considered an opportunity seeker!

So let's say I have a program to sell making money by mailing postcards from home. And let's say I rent a list of 1000 names of opportunity seekers from one of these popular companies. I could get 200 names that answered an ad about raising earthworms for profit. Then maybe another 300 answered an ad about repairing computers for money.

Then maybe 200 answered an ad for growing potted plants for big money. That's 700 of my original 1000 that *probably* will have very, very little interest in my postcard program. WASTED MONEY!

In fact, it's likely that even if the remaining 300 people were interested in some sort of mailing program, most of them are *old* names that won't even bother to give my package a second look! You see, selling names is big business and these companies will keep a name on their list so long as it remains deliverable. My father has not answered an opportunity ad in over *5 years*, yet he still receives offers on a regular basis.

When you see a company that offers what appears to be a large amount of names for a very low price beware. If that same company offers to replace any undeliverable names (known as nixies) you get with 5 or 10 more new names, run for the hills! They're using you to detect their *bad* names and "clean" their list! It costs them next to nothing to send you new names and these "new" names have no guarantee and are probably older than Moses!

So what does all this mean? It means to really get the most out of your mailings you have to be very specific about matching your offer to your list. Opportunity seekers just won't do. If you're offering a network marketing program, get names directly from one of the magazines that promote those programs. Plus, they usually guarantee to pay you $.33 to $.50 for any undeliverable. That's a *real* guarantee! If you offer books on making money in mail order, find a list of known mail order book buyers or even a list of people who do business by mail. If you see someone running ads on a consistent basis that you think their customer list would match your offer, write them and ask what they would charge to rent their list.

Another way is to use the Standard Rate and Data Book, which you can find at your local library. The library can help you with it. There are lists of all kinds of companies and the specific lists that are available. Plus, they tell you the average cost of the item purchased and other valuable information.

Now, I realize a lot of these popular companies advertise that they have many categories of names, but believe me if they're renting them for cheap, they are old, old, over used names that were bought from some dealer. If you go through a broker, they are representing a dealer so you're getting good fresh names and if you're dealing directly with the dealer you should be getting some good prime source names.

Prime source means you're dealing with a company that generated the names from their own advertising. From there, it's easy to just look at the type of ad this company placed to see if your offer matches up well. If the company runs an ad about copying computer disks at home from profit, your postcard program may not do all that well. Even though these people are interested in making money at home, they obviously have a computer and know how to use it. They are probably a little more intelligent (generally speaking) and obviously like using their computer. I'd shop for another list which an appeal closer to the post-card program I'm selling.

This simple revelation dramatically increased the response rate to my direct mail efforts. Now that I've expanded into running ads and help-ing others, this is one of the most valuable concepts I share with people just getting started in this business.

PLAN EVERYDAY

The key to accomplishing a lot is to make a plan *everyday*. A "to do" list with very exact details you want to accomplish. Don't make a list you could never accomplish but make sure you *work your plan*. Just making a list won't get things done. Make a plan *everyday*!!

If you have an overall plan and then just do a small amount each day, you'll be amazed how quickly you'll have the tasks at hand accomplished.

RECOMMENDED READING

I *highly* recommend you find and study these books. They are the absolute best for learning advertising (which is the whole key) and reprogramming your mind for success. If you can't find them at the library, write me and I'll tell you where to order them from.
"How To Write A Good Advertisement"–Victor O. Schwab
        * A must have!
"Tested Advertising Methods"–John Caples
"The Incredible Money Game"–Chuck Rice
        * Another must have!
"Think And Grow Rich"–Napoleon Hill

HOW TO CUT YOUR PRINTING COSTS

You can save 40% to 75% on your printing costs by getting your printing from a mail order printer instead of from your local print shop. The quality can be as good or better than the quality you get from a local printer. Mail order printers advertise in the mail order trade magazines.

Some good ones are listed below. Most can supply you with envelopes as well as circulars.

Budget Signs & Print, 1820 W. Jefferson, Springfield, IL 62702
Domar Printing, 308 Main Street, Laurel, MD 20707
Envelope Sales Company, Normandy, TN 37360
Henry Birtle Co, 1143 E. Colorado Street, Glendale, CA 91205
Lelli Printing, Rt. 2, Loudonville, OH 44842
Mark's Printing Service, PO Box 3408, McKeesport, PA 15134
National, PO Box 1105, Ozark, AL 36361
Sherry Lynn's Printing, 212 W. Main St., Ottawa, IL 61350
Southland Printers, Box 7437R1, Sarasota, FL 33583
Tri Village Printing, 231 Irving Pk Rd, Streamwood, IL 60107

SELLING YOUR PRODUCT IN MAGAZINES–HOW TO WRITE AND DESIGN YOUR OWN ADVERTISEMENTS

You know how to make your own book, you know how to start your own business and you know where and when to advertise. Now you need to know how to sell your product by using small magazine ads.

Selling is nothing more than portraying a product or service in a way that makes it interesting, desirable, necessary, attractive, romantic, provocative, economical, or mysterious. You cannot expect to sell your book by simply placing advertisements that read:

For Sale: A book that explains how to start your own mail order business at home. Send $19.00 to:

John Smith
111 Good Guy Way
Suite 111, Dept. 222
New York, NY 11111

You must create curiosity and desire for your product. You have to make people believe that you have the greatest new idea since sliced bread. Advertisement must make them feel as though they are missing out on a tremendous opportunity if they do not take advantage of your offer.

SOME INTERESTING FACTS ABOUT MAGAZINE ADVERTISING

Magazines are kept longer and reread more often than newspapers, therefore you have more chances of people seeing and reading your ad and making a sale. Also because magazines are kept longer, you may continue to get orders for months after your ad last appeared.

Magazines have a large pass along circulation. Many times people will pass along a magazine to friends, which increases your number of potential customers.

Advertisements in major magazines are often seen as more legitimate than in other publications. The reputation of the magazine sometimes helps the advertisers. Magazines that have a high newsstand circulation as opposed to a large subscription circulation are the best choices. There are two main reasons for this:
People who buy a magazine from a newsstand are buying it because it has interested them and they are almost sure to read it. Many people

who get subscription magazines have lost interest in them and get so many every month that they do not read each one carefully.

You are likely to reach new prospects in a magazine with a high newsstand circulation. Magazines with high newsstand sales are purchased by a wide variety of people. One issue might appeal to one person and not the next and vice-versa. People standing in line at the grocery store will buy a magazine that strikes their interest. Every issue is different and every issue will appeal to different people. You could have millions of new prospects with each issue.

HOW TO DESIGN YOUR OWN SUCCESSFUL CLASSIFIED ADVERTISEMENT

Classifieds can be a good place to start selling your product. Because of the low cost and short lead time involved, classified are very popular for the beginner and old pro alike. They can be an excellent way to test response of a product before jumping into more expensive display advertising.

Classified ads are short so you must condense your sales pitch into a few lines. You must make efficient use of the space if the ad is to be successful. Because there is not enough room to fully explain the value and benefit of a product, it is best not to try and get money out of people with short classified ads unless your product is under $5.00. People are reluctant to risk more than a few dollars on something that they do not know enough about.

Use classified ads to prompt your prospective customers to write or call for more information. When they respond, send them a complete sales letter or brochure that fully explains the features, benefits and guarantees of your product.

HAVE YOUR RESPONSE LETTER READY TO SHIP IMMEDIATELY. DO NOT LET YOUR LEADS GROW COLD

When writing your classified advertisement try to get your message across simply and in a straight forward fashion. Use attention grabbing "buzz" words such as" **New!–Guaranteed!–Secret!–Special!–Limited!–Free!**

Be sure any works you use are accurate and true. You do not want to FTC investigating you. Remember, honesty is the best policy.

The words "book" or "manual" pull much better than instructions or information. Book or manual sound more substantial.

"Free" is a magic word in advertising. Offering "free information" goes a long way even though the free information is your sales letter.

Check the classifieds to find out what other people are doing with their advertisements. If you keep seeing an ad over and over in a newspaper or magazine it usually means it is working. Learn from your competitors. Advertise in publications that already have offers similar to your offer. If other people are selling income opportunities in a publication, the chances are good that yours will sell there too. When you are getting started, it is best to stay on the well traveled road. Do not try publications that no one else is using; it probably means they do not work well. Don't try to pioneer new markets until you can afford it.

Appeal to your prospect's emotions. What drives them, what motives them?

Here's an example of a classified advertisement.

Get Wealthy! Be your own boss! AMAZING new SECRET makes $$ in just days. Free information. Write today! Send SASE John Smith Publishing 111 Good guy Wy. #111A NY, NY 11111

What are the steps involved in getting the prospect to write for more details?

1) Get their attention.

I have used large lettering which is available from many publications in their classified section. Large lettering costs extra but it will catch your potential customer's eye and might make your ad stand out from your competitor's ads.

2) Keep their attention.

Everyone wants to be wealthy, right? And everyone wants to be their own boss.

3) Now throw in some buzz words:

AMAZING–new–SECRET.
You want to build interest and curiosity.

4) Make $$ in days. Quick and easy is the way people like things.

5) Free information keeps them from thinking you are trying to get their money. They can find out more about your offer without sending you a dime.

6) Get them to act.

Now that you have their attention, motivate them to act now. WRITE TODAY! If they put it off they might forget about it.

7) Send S.A.S.E.

This means send a self-addressed stamped enveloped in classified advertising. By requesting that your customer send a self-addressed envelope you will cut down on responses from people who really aren't interested.

Believe it or not, some people are so bored that they will write to anyone and everyone. If you do not ask for a self-addressed stamped envelope you may get a number of responses from people who are just bored and not really interested. If they spend the 33 cents for a stamp and a few cents for an envelope you can be more confident they are a serious prospect. In addition, this will also cut back on paperwork and stamp expenditures for your business.

8) I am sure to include the name of my company so that they know who they are dealing with and I look professional.

9) Address. Remember no PO Boxes. (Not completely important)

10) Because I am either paying per word or per line I have shortened words or used abbreviations whenever possible.

$$ instead of dollars. "Get wealthy! Be your own boss!" instead of "Get wealthy and be your own boss." Wy." In place of Way, "#" instead of number or suite and key the ad with something short like "A", in place of

Dept 222. Many cities also have abbreviations like states, such as NY and LA.

RULES OF BASIC BUSINESS

Now that you are in business, you want to do things properly and give your new business every chance for success.

Don't spend a lot of money until you've done research, testing and planning. Research and planning are essential to the success of any good business. If you jump right into a full page advertisement in a national magazine without test marketing your product and offer, you may lose a lot of money unnecessarily.

Start small. Test your product before buying expensive advertising space. Use classified advertising or small scale direct mailing to promote your product and gage response. If you have a large scale idea you may want to go to your local college and ask a business professor if he can have his students help you with market research. They could be a valuable source of new ideas for marketing and improving your product and advertisements. The fees for such a service are usually very reasonable. If you have the money, you can go to a professional business consultant and retain their services for market research and testing.

Hundreds of businesses fail each year because of poor financial planning. Keep your expenses low and your head out of the clouds. Businesses that grow too fast can find themselves spread too thin and unable to cover their expenses or weather rough times.

When the money starts rolling in, do not rush out and rent an office in a fancy building. Think about the future. Is your product seasonal? Will there be slow periods for your business when there will not be as much money coming in? That big rent payment can kill you if you exhaust the market for one product and need to start promoting another. Always be sure that you will have extra money for the important things when you need it.

One of the most common habits of Americans today is the urge to go out and buy things when we get bored. When people get bored they will buy toys, furniture, new cars, anything to provide some entertainment. They often go into debt to purchase these things and the payment is still around long after the fun has worn off. Be careful not to do this to your business. Don't rush out and get a cellular phone for a status symbol when it is not really necessary to the success of your business. Don't go to your favorite car dealer to buy a business vehicle when your personal car will work ok and provide handsome tax credits for being used as a business vehicle.

REINVESTING PROFITS

The best way to make your money and your business grow is to reinvest as large a portion of your earnings as you can back into the business. If your first ad costs $80.00 and you make $300 net profit then take out a $300.00 ad next time. If the $300.00 ad nets $800.00 profit reinvest as much of it as you can. If you know it is working then there is little risk. Work your way up until you find the most profitable ad sizes. Do not however risk your profits on untried or unsure advertising sources or methods. Test new sources and advertising methods before putting large investments into them.

Cover all of your bases. If you decide to advertise your product in national magazines, find publications that already have offers similar to yours in them. Once you have found a few suitable publications, place small ads in two or more of them. Be sure to key your ad as explained later in this chapter so that you will know which ad is producing the most replies. Then go for larger ads in the magazines that worked the best. Do not spend all of your advertising dollars on one big ad until you have done sufficient testing.

Don't get buried with inventory. The FTC (Federal Trade Commission) requires that you possess a product before you advertise it for sale. Also most advertisers will want a sample of your product before they run your advertisement so that people do not advertise things they cannot supply. Nothing says you have to have a thousand samples on hand. Do not stock up heavy until the orders start coming in.

Keep simple and easy to understand records. General business book-keeping ledgers are available from most office supply stores. Start out immediately with proper bookkeeping. Otherwise you might keep putting it off and before you know it six months have gone by and you cannot remember everything you have done over that period. Bookkeeping is very important for tax purposes. If you have a problem with the IRS they will want to see your bookkeeping.

Keep your receipts. Many things are deductible when you own your own business. But you need to keep receipts of everything that you intend to deduct in case you are audited.

Talk to a tax preparer to find out how much of your earnings you know to set aside for income tax.

If your new business is going to be your sole source of employment, be sure not to get too comfortable with being your own boss. When you are working for yourself, especially when you work at home, it is easy to develop some bad habits. Set regular work hours for yourself. Assign yourself hours that are designated strictly for work, like 8-4 or 9-5. Try not to do housework and other chores during work hours. Stay focused on your work.

KEYING YOUR ADVERTISEMENTS

If you expect to keep an accurate record of the responses from your advertisements, you will need a form of record keeping that will allow you to determine which ad your orders are coming from. Keying is marking your ad in a way that identifies the source of each order as it comes in. Keying an ad is simple. All you need to do is change something on your return address, for instance. Let's say my actual address is:

John Smith
1111 Good Guy Way #111
New York, NY 11111

A keyed ad might look like this:

John Smith Publishing
1111 Good Guy Way
Suite 111, Dept. 222
New York, NY 11111

Department 222 is the key number. For another ad I might change this to Dept. 333 and so on. The use of departments gives your company the appearance of being much larger as well as keying your ads.

Using departments is just one way of keying your ad. I could add an initial to my name, such as:

John A. Smith Publishing

If you are doing classified advertising you might want to use a form of keying that will take up less precious space. Instead of using a suite and dept. number, I can use:

1111 Good Guy Wy. #111A

Or

1111 Good Guy Wy. #111B

#111 is all that I really need to be sure that my mail gets to me. Anything else that I add to my address is just to give my company the appearance of being larger or to key my ads.

The way that you choose to key your ad is not important, but it is important to key them in some way. It is very important that you know exactly where your customer saw the advertisement. If you do not key your ads, you could be paying for two or three ads in different publications not knowing that only one is bringing in responses and the others are a waste of money. You will not know when to stop unproductive ads or step-up ads in productive publications unless you use keys.

You can also use keying to test new and different ads. If you are testing a new offer, you will want to be sure and key it so that you will know if your responses are coming from the new offer or an old offer. Experiment and see what works best.

DEVELOPING YOUR OWN DISTRIBUTOR NETWORK

The first rule to achievement of a fortune is to produce or buy your product for pennies and sell for dollars. So after preliminary market research to determine who will buy your product, the next question to answer is: How much will the majority of this market be willing to pay for your product?

For the sake of our discussion, let's say that you've written a "How-To" manual on how to make $100,000 a year compiling and selling mailing lists. You check with a number of printers and get a production cost of $1.50 per book in lots of 1,000. You figure that with sharp advertising, you can sell a million of these books at $10 per copy, but that advertising will cost you $1.50 per book thus far, the basic cost of your book is $3 per copy.

Even though you will probably be the one selling most of your books, you must realize that it will take you an awfully long time to move out a million copies of this book. It will keep you busy 25 hours a day, 8 days a week to do it all by yourself. So the thing to do is recruit as many other people as you can to help do the selling. This means setting up a dealer distributor network.

To do this, you must make it worthwhile for other people to sell your product. You offer a percentage of the sales price on each book they sell for you. Generally, this is about 50% for each single copy sold; 60% when purchased in quantity lots of 25 to 99 copies; and 75% when purchased in lots of 100 or more. The important thing is to shave your profits to a minimum when you have other people doing the work for you.

Let's use, then, our example of a $10 book that costs you $1.50 to produce in lots of 1,000. For people who buy from you in lots of 100 copies, you could cut your profits to $1 per book, sell it to them for $2.50 per book and let them do all the advertising, as well as the selling. Don't offer more than 50% on single copy drop-ship sales, because you'll have to furnish this type of dealer with selling materials, and continue to do most of the advertising yourself.

Setting up your distributor program will require an advertising and sales kit for the sellers. Thus, you should make up a series of "dealers wanted" ads and place them in as many different publications as you can.

The national "opportunity" magazines are the best place to place your advertising for dealers. Remember, the ad should be a call for dealers, distributors and independent extra income seekers. Do not try to sell your product in this ad. Use it only to enlist or recruit people to sell for you. Remember too, the more you run your dealers wanted ad, and the more different publications you run it in, the more people you'll get to sell your product for you. The easiest way to go is the "Dealers Wanted" advertisements in as many worldwide publications as possible.

To actually get these interested opportunity seekers to sell your product for you, you'll need a dynamic sales letter and seller's kit to send out in response to the replies to your advertising. This kind of sales letter is usually four pages in length, printed on 11 by 17 inch paper, and then folded in half, book style. But if it takes 10 or more pages to sell the prospect on the idea of selling for you, use the amount of space and paper that's necessary.

In addition to your sales letter, you should have at least three camera-ready ads the opportunity seeker can use to advertise your product. These should include a classified ad, a one-inch display ad, and a larger

2-column by 3-inch ad with blank spaces for him to insert his own name and address. You should also include at least one full-page camera-ready circular he can use as an "original" in ordering printing of his own direct mail circulars.

This is how you set up a dealer/distributor network: Get other people to sell your product for you! You can, and should be prepared from the start, before you place your first dealers wanted ad, and proceed only as you can afford the advertising costs from the profits of sales of your product.

PUTTING IT ALL TOGETHER

I want to stress to you that you will make more money when you put together your own project and sales letter! What this is all about being completely self dependent, self reliant. Build something fresh and new that no one's seen before. I'm getting you started just like I did, taking you under my wing and showing you how it's done. The last step is yours…

Many beginners quit before they get going long enough to make money. Part of it is unrealistic expectations generated by some mail order advertisers. Contrary to popular belief, you cannot get rich doing almost nothing. But that doesn't mean you can't make good money with some honest effort. People fail to make money in this business because they choose not to put any serious effort into it. Some mail as few as 50 poorly folded letters then quit. People give up because they don't make any money after 2 hours of work! They quit because they invested $80 and lost it all. Meanwhile, they haven't read a single book on the subject! GET REAL!! People spend thousands of dollars and four years at college before they get a cent back! And most of them don't make as much money as I do working from my kitchen table! When I first started, I spent at least $200 on mail order and advertising books and courses. I invested thousands in advertising, printing, and postage. And I worked over 20 hours a week before I began to see a profit! I could see that others had made great money in mail order and I was determined to find out how. Luckily, a few of them took me under their wing and showed me the ropes…much like I'm doing here for you. I've literally saved you thousands of dollars in trial and error by sharing my secrets with you. But I can't do it for you! Your journey will not be nearly as hard as mine. Once I learned the secrets I've shared here with you, I was able to show people how to get started much quicker and easier than I did. Yet, it still takes a serious effort on your part. It takes more than mailing 100 flyers and then expecting a flood of money in your mailbox.

Chapter Six

The MLM Crash Coarse

HOW TO CREATE A CASH EXPLOSION IN YOUR MAILBOX!

Believe it or not, there are many ordinary people making from $10,000 to $50,000 a MONTH in mail order as we speak. Maybe you've seen or read about these people. How are they doing it? What's their SECRET?

Their SECRET is Network Marketing. Commonly known as Multi Level Marketing or MLM for short. Most of the Ultra BIG earners in mail order are involved in Networking by mail. They've built large sales organizations without any employees, inventory and very little overhead. Most of them work in the comfort of their homes, their vacation retreats or wherever they want to work. There are NO physical restrictions in this type of business.

Personally, I used to HATE network marketing. You had to chase your friends and family, attend pep rallies and cold call perfect strangers who would think you're some kind of nut. Well, things have changed drastically! For the BETTER I might add!

In the year 2000, it's now possible to build a HUGE Networking business without ever meeting your distributor face to face. Modern day miracles such as the Internet, 800 phone lines, conference calls, audio cassettes, video tapes and on and on, allow us to communicate with people from around the globe one on one. Modern Networking is simply an incredible way to generate enormous sums of money. And the best part, virtually anyone with a little drive and work ethic can succeed. It's been said that there are NO failures in Networking, only quitters.

In case you're not sure what Network Marketing really is, or how it works, let me teach you some of the basics.

TWO TYPES OF INCOME!

There are TWO types of income everyone of us could earn. Linear income and Residual income. LINEAR INCOME is where you trade your time for money. You work at your job and get paid for your time at regular intervals. This is the type of income MOST of us earn. Linear income is very important because it provides the CASH FLOW you need to pay your expenses However, it's very limiting because you are primarily relying on your own efforts. There are only so many hours in a day, week or month in which you can work.

RESIDUAL INCOME is the type of income that could make you RICH! It's your rainy day money. This is where you do your work one time and get paid again and again. Singers, songwriters, actors and authors all earn RESIDUAL INCOME. Every time someone buys their CD or book, or watches their TV show, they earn money. Some Cable TV Channels show nothing but reruns of shows that were popular decades ago. The actors earn residuals every time their movie or show is aired. Sometimes, their ESTATES earn income for years after the stars are dead. The POWER of residual income is that it can go on and on long after you've stopped working.

Thanks to Network Marketing, you don't have to be a popular singer, songwriter or actor to enjoy the benefits of RESIDUAL INCOME!

Network Marketing has this incredible potential because it allows you to build a HUGE sales organization, with just a few people to start with. This is possible because of the POWER of Geometric Progression or DOUBLING. For instance, you can start off with four people and teach them how to find four each, and without any extra effort on your part, you have 20 people in your organization. At some point, those 20 can become 40, 80, 160 and more. And YOU earn money on the efforts of each of them. This allows you to do your work once, and get paid over and over again.

Let me give you an example of the enourmous POWER of doubling.

If I were to ask you which you would rather have, $100,000 NOW…or a penny that doubles everyday for 31 days…how would you answer?

If you're like most people…you would take the money and run. There was a time when I would have too. However, by doing so, you would have lost over 10 MILLION dollars! You can do the math yourself and see how a penny doubled every day for 31 days adds up to $$$$$$$$

Now which you would rather have, $100,000 or ten MILLION dollars?…I'm pretty sure I know the answer to that. Do you see the POWER of geometric progression at work here? It's nothing more than a doubling effect. Only in Networking, we're not doubling pennies, we're doubling PEOPLE! It's commonly called DUPLICATION!
Instead of being paid ONLY on your efforts…(Linear Income)…you are also being paid on the efforts of many different people working for you. Every time these people earn money, so do you without lifting a finger. Every time one of them adds a new recruit, YOU get the benefit

of the growth as well as they. When YOU stop working…you get paid as long as the others below you do their work.

Network marketing is truly a brilliant form of compensation because it rewards you not only for your efforts, but for the efforts of every one in your organization under you. With our doubling effect, there can be hundreds or even thousands of people working for YOU.

The BIG money makers of mail order have simply learned to TAP into this incredible cash cow called Networking.

If you want to be one of the BIG money earners of mail order and make Networking your primary business…there are a few basic things you should know before you jump in.

BEWARE OF SCHEMES DISGUISED AS MLM!

In mail order circles, Network marketing is often confused with Chain Letters, Money Games and Ponzi Schemes. Many mail order operators tack on any old product, add a multi tiered compensation plan and call it MLM. They make promises of great wealth, easy money and paint rosy pictures of spending 30 minutes mailing offers, and lounging in the sun the rest of the day. All the while, the cash just floods into the mailbox.

In reality, nothing could be farther from the truth. If you aren't careful, it's easy to fall into the Easy Riches traps that some clever copywriters devise.

A genuine Networking business offers a fairly priced, legitimate product that appeals to a large group of people. They don't promise quick or instant riches and they are operated by a legitimate company with *a real staff of people to assist you.*

Our whole economy is based on the movement of goods and services to the end consumer. Mail order and networking through the mail is no different.

So, before you become involved in any mail order MLM, beware and make sure you're dealing with a legitimate company that offers REAL products you would be willing to sell to your best friend if you had to. The BIG money earners and NOT playing money games.

DO YOUR HOMEWORK WHEN CHOOSING A COMPANY! DUE DILIGENCE!

I'm told at any given time there are more than 3,000 Networking opportunities available. Probably *less than 200* of them are worthy of any serious consideration.

One of the most basic things to watch for is the *age* of the company. According to the Direct Marketing Association, over 90% of all START UP MLM companies go out of business within their first TWO years! Another percentage close down before their fifth birthday. So, I wouldn't recommend investing in any company less than five years old. Also, what about the management team? Do they have a successful track record with other businesses? Are the company managers accessible? Are they willing to provide you with a sufficient amount of information to allow you to make a reasonable buying decision? If not, stay away.

Before you make a financial commitment to your MLM company, try their products to determine if they are something you would be happy to offer others. After all, it all comes down to product. Make sure the products appeal to a large group of people. If you're products are of interest to a limited group of buyers...you will have a harder time selling them. For example, you could be the best Pet Rock manufacturer on earth. However, if the market for your product is limited, you will have a hard time selling your rocks.

The *bottom line* is this when choosing your company. If you were the last distributor to join the company, could you sell the products without the opportunity attached? If not, run for the hills.

PROMOTING YOUR NEW COMPANY!

Once you've decided which company is right for you, it's time to start promoting.

Since this book is about "mail order," I'm going to show you the BEST way to promote your MLM company through the mail. These methods have worked for me and many others.

SEVEN BASIC SECRETS TO SUCCESS IN NET-WORKING BY MAIL!

1. Cash FLOW! Remember my earlier examples of Linear and Residual Income? Residual Income can make you RICH. However, when you're first starting your business, you're still going to need a source of CASH FLOW to allow you to *build*

your residual income. It's going to take a while to generate sufficient residual income to survive. So, you MUST make sure you have another source of income that is adequate to finance your new operation and continue to maintain your standard of living. The best time to start an MLM is when you are gainfully employed and have a steady source of income. If you wait until you're unemployed, it may be too late.

2. **Goals!** Goal setting is one of the most important aspects of business success. Decide how much YOU want to make, then, have a PLAN that will allow you to accomplish those goals. Once you understand your companies compensation plan, figure out how many distributors you will need in your organization to make the type of income you're looking for. Experience will teach you how quickly you can accomplish your goals. Set them in easy STEPS! For instance, maybe your goal is to sign up your first four distributors within one month. If you don't accomplish this, do some trouble shooting and find out what went wrong. What could you have done better? Maybe your goals were unrealistic…or you didn't put the effort in that YOU had originally planned. If so, simply adjust your goals to make them achievable.

3. **Commitment!** Learn right now that there is NO way to get rich QUICK! Building a business requires time, effort and a great deal of VISION in order to succeed. Even when working through the mail. People who succeed in MLM are no different than those who succeed in any other traditional business. They are committed to their business and work hard to insure their success. Be willing to commit at least TWO YEARS of hard work if necessary, just to get your business off the ground.

4. **Qualify Your Prospects!** Don't waste too much time or money working with people who aren't committed to your business.

You will quickly learn that many people only THINK they want to build a business. What they're really looking for is a handout or for someone else to make a living for them. One way to qualify prospects is to keep the HYPE to a minimum. Let your prospect know up front he will have to work to be successful.

5. **Have A Marketing System in place for Non Sales Types!** You may be the greatest sales person to walk the face of the earth. There's a good chance, however, that most of your distributors won't be. In fact, 95% of all MLM prospects hate selling. Before your prospect will join your company, he must be totally convinced that he can do your business. So, if you want to build a large sales organization, you MUST provide him with an easy way to duplicate YOUR efforts without SELLING! One of the most popular methods of recruiting today is to refer prospects to a professional Opportunity Line that does the selling for you. I've personally used this system and it works. Teach your prospects to find leads, and let the 800# do most of the selling.

6. **Training!** Your system must supply the TRAINING your new recruit needs. In the beginning, you may be willing to do most of the work for a newcomer. Sooner or later, however, he will have to learn to do for himself. He needs to know where to find leads, what to mail and when to mail it. Also, even though he may do little personal selling, there's no way he can avoid talking to people at some point in his career. MLM is a people business. So, he needs to understand BASIC communication skills.

7. **Stay Focused!** One of the best things you can do for yourself and your new recruit is to help them stay focused on their goals. Once your distributor loses focus, he is destined to fail. A distributor in one Networking company tells her recruits to pick out the house of their dreams, then drive by it everyday and

pretend their going home. This keeps them reminded of what they hope to someday accomplish.

Now that you have an understanding of the basics, let me give you a SPECIFIC method that I and others have used to build our business through the mail.

Experience has taught me that the BEST way to sell an MLM program is on the BACK END of something else. Preferably an inexpensive money making report, book or cassette.

You could purchase or compile a small report or booklet that shows your prospects why they need your MLM opportunity...and how they can benefit from it. The real purpose of the report is to do a selling job on your prospect. Give the report a clever title that promises to divulge some money making SECRET or idea. For instance, *HOW TO MAKE $50,000 A YEAR In MLM Without Selling Or Chasing Your Friends!*

Offer the report for $3 to $5. Write a small ad to promote it and have it typeset on an inexpensive postcard. Later, you can even place it in newspapers or large opportunity magazines. Limit the number of words in your ad. The best ads combine Opportunity with MYSTERY! Curiosity COMPELS your prospect to order the report. With small ads, LESS is more. If you provide too much information, he may not order the report. If you present too little information, you may get the wrong type of prospect. The key is to balance the two.

Once you have your postcard professionally typeset and printed, mail it to a list of MLM buyers and instruct them to purchase the report directly from you.

When someone orders your report, simply send it to them along with a personal letter written and signed by you. Make sure your letter is on professional letterhead. It doesn't hurt to also include a business card with your mailing.

You have accomplished three things by doing this. 1) You have generated a small amount of CASH FLOW to help pay for your mailing costs. 2) You have found a future prospect for your MLM opportunity. 3) And…if done properly, you have gained the TRUST of your prospect.

In my opinion, TRUST is the single most important selling point YOU have. You are not only selling your opportunity, you are also selling YOURSELF! Business is NOT just about products and opportunity. It's about PEOPLE. We want to do business with people we know and trust. The report you just sold to your prospect has accomplished your objectives. They know you, they trust you and hopefully you have established your credibility with a stranger.

If your report is compelling enough, your prospect will call YOU and want to join your program or buy your other products. If not, wait 10 days and send another offer. *Don't forget to do the follow up.* Remember, the same rules that apply to ALL businesses apply to direct mail as well. It sometimes takes 3 to 7 follow ups to make the BIG sale.

When your prospect joins your MLM, teach him to do the same thing you did. That will allow him to easily *duplicate* your efforts. When he makes money, so will you.

...*FREE REPORTS!*...

Another way to build credibility is by giving away a *free report* or product sample.

The idea is to get enough free items circulating and hope some of the recipients will see the value of your product or program and buy it. This is a bit risky because it's hard to qualify your prospects with FREE offers. You can lessen the risk by wording your ad to appeal to serious prospects only. For instance, instead of saying...7 FREE SECRETS that Will Make You RICH! Say something like...**FREE REPORT! Seven Ways To Get Rich Using A Telephone!** If you're looking for sales people, this might keep your phone shy prospects away.

Don't you want as many responses as possible? No...not really. It's better to get 10 SERIOUS responses a week than 100 bad responses. Remember, you're looking for SERIOUS people. If you're trying to sell a LEGITIMATE program, forget the non committed ones.

When giving away FREE reports or samples, it's important to capture your prospects phone number along with the name and address. Professional marketers will almost always make a follow up phone call to see if the prospect is interested in their MLM offer. Regardless of how you follow up with your prospect, it is very important to the marketing process. Either by mail or phone.

Other easy ways to generate cash flow while you build your business.

The same report or booklet you sold to your prospect, can also be sold to their downline. Offer the product at a fair wholesale price if purchased in quantities. Then, when your downline sells them, they can make a small profit on each sale and help pay for the expense of their mailing too. This gives both YOU and your downline every opportunity to succeed.

Another way to generate cash flow is by selling quality mailing lists to other marketers. If you place ads or do a lot of mailing, sell the names who have responded but haven't purchased your program. All you need is a well written flyer that explains how good your names are, and why others should use them. You could also sell printing to your downline members. There are several wholesale printers who will do the work for you at reduced pricing. Just mark up the printing to standard retail and that's your profit.

There are MANY ways to generate cash flow that will enable you to offset your promotional expenses. Provide your people with a way to stay in business and build a downline of their own...and with MLM, you could become very wealthy indeed!

Response rates.

There are two types of response rates you should know about. Inquiry rates and sales conversion rates. When someone requests more information, that's an inquiry. Inquiry rates are generally much higher than sales rates. A good ad can generate a 5 % inquiry rate. On the other hand, the number of inquiries you convert to sales will be much lower. Typically, sales conversion rates average from ½ to 1%.

Mailing Lists!

Before you do large numbers of mailings, test your list first. Professionals generally purchase lists in quantities of 1000 or more names. However, before they mail to all of them, they will test at least 20% at random. If the response is what they expected, they will mail to the remainder of the list. If not, they will usually discard the remainder of the names and test another list.

When testing lists, it's very important to mail the *same identical offer* to each list. If all of your tests yield poor results, the problem could be the offer. The only way to know is to make changes to the sales material or ads and start testing again.

The BEST lists are those of your own customer base. If someone has purchased from you before, they are likely to do so again. If you're new to the business, you will have to place ads or rent mailing lists to develop a customer base.

What about mailing cassettes, videos or expensive brochures?

Many beginning networkers start their careers by mailing company marketing materials to COLD lists. However, most people who do this aren't very successful.

The BEST method is to generate cash flow first, build trust…then sell your MLM on the BACK END as I have discussed here. When care is taken to do it properly, the rewards can be astounding!

You could be the next $50,000 a month earner in Network Marketing.

Epilogue

Using the techniques put forth in this book can make you a lot of money, they've been proven by us and many others over and over again. The key is to take your time, do your homework and put in the effort to make it happen.

Our most sincerest wish is that this book has *empowered* you to start a business and make your dreams come true. No one can do it for you but others will do it instead of you if you don't take the bull by the horns and do it.

Roger and I have joined forces and developed a complete marketing system based on the methods we've revealed to you here. If you would like a free introductory package outlining our program and payouts, please write:

Roger Mason
c/o Mason Marketing Group   or   www.lancemurkin.com
PO Box 333
Energy, IL 62933

About the Authors

Roger Mason is a former accountant and business adviser turned professional marketer. Along with his wife Kathy, he operates his own home-based direct marketing company, MASON MARKETING.

Prior to starting his home business, Roger did a 10-year stint as the Audit Manager of a CPA firm and later as Chief Executive Officer of a Health Care organization. Roger holds Bachelors degrees in Business and Photojournalism and finds that working from home is the greatest thrill in life.

Lance Murkin is an acclaimed singer/songwriter, father of two and a full-time student of life. He is a regular featured columnist in *MAIL ORDER MARKETING NEWS* and a contributor to most of the major home business and money making magazines available today. From his home outside Kansas City, he operates REAL WEALTH PUBLICA-TIONS which he started literally right from his kitchen table. After seven years in the printing business and four years managing a bowling pro shop, he went on his quest to make money working from home and says this business has given him a level of financial and emotional freedom he is grateful for every day of his life.

Appendix

THE MAIL ORDER INFORMATION RESOURCE GUIDE

WHERE TO FIND PRODUCTS

Following are companies that offer drop ship and/or dealership opportunities for information books, reports, directories and more:

Variety Publications (money-making and home-based business manuals, reports, books, etc.) PO Box 400597, Brooklyn, NY 11240-0597

Premier Publishers (over 600 books, reports, manuals and more) PO Box 330309, Ft. Worth, TX 76163-0309

NBR (over 700 guides, books, etc. drop shipping available) Box 33923, San Antonio, TX 78265

Selective Books (trade directories and mail order books) PO Box 1140, Clearwater, FL 34617

Allen Publishing Co. (books and manuals–drop shipping available) PO Box 371900, Reseda, CA 91337

Mascor Publishing Co. (tapes, books, CD's–drop shipping available) PO Box 110, Laurel, MD 20725

Publishers Media (1000% profit selling reports & manuals) PO Box 1295, El Cajon, CA 92022-1295

Stew Caverly (reprintable reports & manuals) 216 McLean St., Wilkes-Barre, PA 18702-4573

North American Booksellers Exchange (loaded with wholesale/drop ship offers. Sample copy $3) PO Box 606, Cottage Grove, OR 97424

American Drop-Shippers Directory (wholesale drop shipping guide–thousands of companies) Dolphin Publishing Group, PO Box 2570, Fair Oaks, CA 95628-2570

Unless noted, you need to send a S.A.S.E. to the above companies to receive the information. They will provide you with information on the products and services they provide.

MAIL ORDER PRINTING COMPANIES

These local companies can print your booklets, reports, manuals or books–also check your local print shops:

- *Night and Day Printing,* PO Box 700, Baldwin Park, CA 91706
- *Budget Printing,* 2765-H West Jefferson, Springfield, IL 62702
- *Lelli Printing,* 2650 CR 175, Loudonville, OH 44842
- *Advance Printers,* 705 S. Union, Ozark, AL 36361
- *USA Printing,* 160 Washington SE, Suite 30, Albuquerque, NM 87108

- *Prime Publishers,* Inc., PO Box 680, Swainsboro, GA 30401

MAILING LIST PROVIDERS

You can check your local phone directory for mailing list brokers. You should also check out STANDARD RATE AND DATA SERVICE (SRDS)–available at any library. This source lists thousands of lists available, list brokers, and other information. These companies offer mailing lists for a variety of categories.

TJT Marketing Associates, PO Box 55685, Valencia, CA 91385 Ph: (661) 291-1289

- *TJT Marketing Associates,* PO Box 55685, Valencia, CA 91385 Ph: (661) 291-1289
- *All Media, Inc.,* 4965 Preston Park Blvd., #300, Plano, TX 75093
- *Names Unlimited,* 345 Park Ave. South, New York, NY 10010
- *Unimail List Corp.,* 1701 E. Lake Avenue, Glenview, IL 60025
- *WMI/Worldata,* 5200 Town Center, Boca Raton, FL 33486
- *Hugo Dunhill Lists,* Inc., 630 3rd Avenue, New York, NY 10017
- *The Kaplan Agency,* 1200 High Ridge Road, Stamford, CT 06905
- *Charles Crane Associates,* 2050 Center Avenue, Ft. Lee, NJ 07024

PRINT & MAIL DEALERS

These companies will print and mail your full page circulars and ads either via First Class Mail or Bulk Mail. Contact them for samples of their mailings.

- *Carl T. O'Shea,* PO Box 700, Baldwin Park, CA 91706
- *Adams Publications,* Box 35718, Fayetteville, NC 28303
- *Chuck Rollason,* PO Box 370, Dauphin, PA 17018
- *Profit Gems Marketing,* POB 3087, Jekyll Island, GA 31527

WHERE TO ADVERTISE

These are smaller "inner circle" type mail order publications:

- *Jackpot*, PO Box 6547, Jacksonville, FL 32236-6547
- *Mail Order Messenger*, PO Box 358, Middleton, TN 38052
- *The Biz-Ness Gazette*, PO Box 4225, Elkhart, IN 46514-4225
- *G&B Records*, PO Box 10150, Terra Bella, CA 93270-0150
- *Profit Gems*, PO Box 3087, Jekyll Island, GA 31527
- *Phoenix 5000*, 1051 Foxchase Lane, Baltimore, MD 21221
- *Emerald Coast News*, 21 Racetrack Road NE, Fort Walton Beach, FL 32547
- *Mail Order Network Newsletter*, PO Box 700, Baldwin Park, CA 91706
- *Ben Frank's Almanac*, PO Box 655, Pinellas Park, FL 33780
- *The American Banner*, Box 263154, Tampa, FL 33685
- *Budget Advertiser*, 2765-H W. Jefferson, Springfield, IL 62702
- *Gumball Express*, 12 Westerville Sq. #149, Westerville, OH 43081
- *Money Makers Monthly*, 643 Executive Dr., Willowbrook, IL 60521
- *National Advertiser*, PO Box 624, Cherokee Village, AR 72525
- *Spotlight*, 1504 Hwy 15, L2, Myrtle Beach, SC 29577

You should also look into the larger circulation publications. Once again, write to them and request a media kit. Some of the better publications for placing money making advertisements are:

- *The Enquirer*, Lantana, FL 33464
- *The Star*, Box 1510, Clearwater, FL 34617
- *Income Opportunities*, 1000 Broadway, New York, NY 10036

- *Money Making Opportunities*, 11071 Ventura Blvd., Studio City, CA 91604
- *Extra Income*, PO Box 21957, Santa Barbara, CA 93121
- *Spare Time*, 5810 West Oklahoma Ave., Milwaukee, WI 53219-4384
- *Popular Mechanics*, 224 W. 57th St., New York, NY 10019
- *Grit*, 208 W. Third, Williamsport, PA 17701
- *Capper's Weekly*, 616 Jefferson St., Topeka, KS 66607
- *Classified, Inc.*, 100 E. Ohio St., Chicago, IL 60611 (handle many different publications)
- *National Mail Order Classified*, PO Box 2581, Birmingham, AL 35202
- *Small Business Opportunities*, 1115 Broadway, New York, NY 10010
- *Business Opportunities Journal*, PO Box 60762, San Diego, CA 92106-8762
- *Entrepreneur*, 2392 Morse Avenue, Irvine, CA 92714
- *New Business Opportunities*, PO Box 50347, Boulder, CO 80321
- *Business Start-Ups*, 2392 Morse Ave., Irvine, CA 9271
- *Home Business Magazine*, 9582 Hamilton Ave., Suite 368, Huntington Beach, CA 92646
- *Home Business Connection*, Cutting Edge Media, 29 South Market St., Elizabethtown, PA 17022
- *Opportunity World*, 28 Vesey St., #257, New York, NY 10007
- *Wealth Building*, 15738 S. Bell Rd., Suite 200, Lockport, 60441
- *Money N' Profits*, 28 Vesey St., New York, NY 10007

Contact any of the aforementioned publications, and ask them for a sample issue and advertising rate information. Most will send a sample of the publication. If they do not, ask them for a copy of the classified pages from the *Money Making Opportunities* or *Business Opportunities* sections.

www.ingramcontent.com/pod-product-compliance
Lightning Source LLC
Chambersburg PA
CBHW030819180526
45163CB00003B/1346